The Barefoot Boys of Fayette

Regene Henry

Illustrated by
Carolyn R. Stich

EDCO Publishing, Inc.
2648 Lapeer Rd.
Auburn Hills, MI 48326
www.edcopublishing.com

Printed in the United States of America

ISBN: 0-9749412-3-9

For Judy Parlato -
friend, proofreader, encourager,
and fellow U.P. history lover.

R.H.

For the Michigan State Parks
which have provided my family
with many wonderful memories
year after year.

C.R.S.

Snail Shell Harbor
Fayette Historic State Park

Historic Fayette

Chapter 1
(The Present)

As the big yellow bus rolled down highway U.S. 2, Ty Carlson leaned his head against the fogged window glass and wondered what this field-trip day would be like.

He knew, because his older brother Adam had told him at breakfast, that the fourth-grade teachers always took their classes to the state park at Fayette for a field trip in the fall. "You'll learn about a lot of state parks in Michigan history class, but learning about Fayette is the best because you get to go there and see what it's like," Adam had told him.

"What is it like?" he had asked.

"It's cool. They've got old buildings all fixed up and a great beach and cliffs. I think there are caves in the cliffs, but I never got the chance to check them out because I had Mrs. Torrence-the-Terrible for my fourth-grade teacher. She didn't let us out of her eagle-eye sight all day long."

1

Ty nodded. Mrs. Torrence had retired last year, just in time, as far as Ty was concerned, so he didn't have to worry about getting assigned to her class. Instead, he had Mr. Munson who was young enough to remember and understand what it was like to be a kid. He was pretty sure Mr. Munson wouldn't watch him with an eagle eye all day. He hoped not, because there were some things Adam had said this morning that he wanted to check out. The caves, for instance. And something else, something kind of strange.

"In fact," Adam had continued, "the weirdest thing happened. Fayette is a ghost town, you know, and I think I saw some of them, the ghosts."

Ty stopped shoveling Cheerios into his mouth and looked at his brother. "What? Are you crazy? There's no such thing as ghosts. Everybody knows that."

"That's what I always thought, too, until that day in the hotel at Fayette." Adam concentrated on spreading peanut butter right up to the edges of the crusts of his toast.

Ty waited, going crazy, for Adam to continue his story. But Adam concentrated on his toast. Now he was slicing a banana and carefully arranging the slices on top of the peanut butter. Finally, Ty couldn't stand waiting. "C'mon, Adam, tell me!"

"Tell you what?" Adam took a bite out of

his toast and chewed slowly.

Ty took in a big breath. He knew that Mom always told them they shouldn't talk with food in their mouths, so now he would have to wait until Adam swallowed. He exhaled loudly. Adam grinned, peanut butter-banana mush showing on his teeth. Gross. Ty knew his brother was annoying him on purpose. He decided to pretend it wasn't bothering him. He concentrated on his Cheerios again. They were beginning to get soggy. Ty hated soggy cereal.

Finally, Adam took a big gulp of milk, wiped his hand across his mouth, and began his story. "I was in the hotel there at Fayette. They have it all fixed up so it looks like it did back in the 1800s. I was near the front doorway, inside the room, looking over at the desk where visitors would register. I was just standing there, thinking about how different it was than hotels are nowadays. Then I thought I saw someone, or something, behind the desk. It was a man in a white shirt, with suspenders and a sun visor thing on his forehead. Kind of wavery. Like I could sort of see him, but I could also sort of see through him, too. It was weird. Then I heard a tinkling laugh, and I glanced to the left in the room, over by the window, and I thought I saw a lady in a long, brown dress and a hat with a big, curly feather. She was sort of see-through-ee, too. Then Torrance-the-Terrible blew her whistle, and one of the guys came running in and grabbed my arm and started pulling me out of the room. I looked at him. When I looked back into the room, no one was there." Adam shrugged and took another bite of his toast. "It kind of gave me the creeps," he said, chewing thoughtfully.

"Are you telling me the truth? Or are you just trying to weird me out?" Ty asked.

"That's really the way it was. Scout's honor," Adam said.

If Adam said "scout's honor," Ty would believe him. Adam was really into scouting. He was determined to be an eagle scout someday and was constantly working toward badges. An eagle scout wanna-be wouldn't use "scout's honor" to tell a lie. Ty felt a shivery feeling. Ghosts! Adam really thought there were ghosts at Fayette and he'd seen them. Wow!

So now, in the big yellow bus, rolling down the road, Ty kept watch out the window, waiting for his first glimpse of the townsite of Fayette. He wondered if maybe, just possibly, he might see the ghosts, too.

Fayette Townsite

Historical Fayette

Chapter 2

They'd spent hours touring the village of Fayette. The teachers and the state park historian had taken them all around the town, told them all the history, let them go inside the buildings. They saw the big limestone building with its tall furnace smoke stacks, where iron ore had been smelted, or melted, and formed into bars, called pig iron. Funny name, Ty thought. They saw the stage of the music hall, draped in red, white, and blue, as if a show were planned for that very evening. They saw red plastic meats and sausages in the butcher shop and antique barber tools in the barber shop. They saw the mining company's ledger books in the paymaster's office, the big white house where the furnace superintendent had lived, and the smaller brick house up the road where the town's doctor had lived. They walked to a small wood cabin, like the ones where the furnace laborers and their families once lived. The kids were amazed at how tiny it was, just a kitchen and living room downstairs and a sloped ceiling room up a narrow set of stairs where the whole family slept. Ty couldn't imagine living in such a cramped space. He knew his family's couch and recliners and large screen T.V. would never fit in this small space.

One of the kids' favorite places was the building dedicated to what it was like to be a child in the town of Fayette before it was abandoned. There were old-fashioned toys and games, books, and very uncomfortable-looking clothes and shoes. And they saw the downstairs rooms of the hotel.

One building contained several pictures and posters. Ty's favorite picture was blown up into a large poster. It showed all the workers lined up in front of the blast furnace in their old-fashioned, dirty-looking clothes. And in front of the workers stood a group of boys, all barefoot except for one.

"We call this photo 'The Barefoot Boys,'" the park historian explained. "We are all fascinated with the picture, but we have never been able to find out who the boys were or why they were included in the photo." Ty looked more closely at the barefoot boys, especially at their faces. If he ignored their old-fashioned clothes and just concentrated on their faces, he thought, they looked a lot like kids he knew. He wondered if, hundreds of years into the future, kids might see a picture of him and his friends and wonder about them. It was interesting to think about.

Everywhere he went in the village, Ty watched very closely and listened even closer, especially at the the hotel, but he neither saw nor heard anything ghostly. He stood in the exact spot he thought Adam had stood in at the entrance to the hotel's lobby. He stared at the reception desk. He listened for a lady's laugh. Nothing. He was disappointed.

Later, he and his best friend Eric sat on the wooden dock at the harbor's edge eating their sack lunches, looking across the small harbor to the white cliffs on the other side.

"Mr. Munson is giving us some exploration time later, Eric," Ty said. "My brother says there are caves over there in the cliffs. Want to go exploring with me?"

"Sure," Eric agreed.

*   *   *   *   *

"Okay, kids," Mr. Munson said later. "You have one hour of free exploration time. Use your common sense and have fun. We'll toot the bus horns when it's time to leave." The kids ran off in all directions—some to further explore the village's buildings, some to the gift shop and the model of the village they'd seen in the Visitors' Center, and some to the picnic area and beach. Ty and Eric headed toward the white cliffs.

"'Common sense,' Mr. Munson said. Are you sure we are using our common sense?" Eric asked as he followed Ty on a narrow path along the bottom of the cliffs, a few feet above the water.

"You worry too much," Ty said, laughing. "Let's see how far we can get in half and hour. Then we'll turn back. Who knows? Maybe we'll discover a pirate's cave."

"I don't think there were pirates on Lake Michigan," Eric said.

"You never know," Ty said. "Maybe we'll find out."

When Ty next looked at his watch, twenty minutes had passed. Ten more and they'd have to turn back. Ty put his hand up to his forehead to act as a visor for his eyes. He let his eyes travel ahead and upward, surveying the cliffs. He thought he saw something. "Look!" He pointed to a ledge a few feet above the path and about a hundred feet ahead of them. "See that dark crack up there? I bet it's a cave. C'mon."

"I bet it's just a crack," Eric grumbled as he followed.

When they reached the spot directly below

the ledge, Ty stretched his head back as far as he could to see, but he couldn't. They were too close, directly under the ledge, to see what was above it.

"I don't think we can get up there," Eric said.

"I can. Just give me a boost."

"Okay. It's your funeral." Eric shrugged. "Be careful. I'd really hate to have to go back and tell Mr. Munson that you fell off the cliff and drowned in the lake."

"Quit worrying and boost me up."

Ty reached to grab at rocks above him while Eric pushed him from below. He found a few good footholds and handholds and scrambled up to the ledge. Once up on top, he smiled down at Eric. "You want to come up?"

"No. How are you gonna get down?" Eric wanted to know.

Ty ignored him. "I think it is a cave! There is an opening in the cliffs!" he shouted excitedly.

"It's probably full of bats," Eric warned.

Ty didn't care. He was overcome with curiosity and the excitement of exploring.

He entered the cave and found it full of dampness and dusk-like dark. He yelled to Eric, "It's big!" But his voice echoed so loudly against the rock walls that he covered his ears with his hands against the reverberating sound.

Cautiously, he stepped forward, each foot carefully placed. After a few minutes, his eyes became adjusted to the darkness, and he could see darker shadows in the dimness. He stopped when he heard Eric's voice which sounded very far away. The only word he heard was "time." It was probably time to head back to the busses, he figured, but he couldn't stop now. He just couldn't, especially when he thought he saw something square on the stone floor ahead of him. He wished he had a flashlight.

As he got closer, Ty could see that it was some sort of box, a dark wooden box, about the size of the box his dad's new boots had come in. It was covered with a layer of dirt and dust. He brushed his hand over the top, and a cloud of dust rose, making him sneeze. "Ah-choo!"

Bending to see if he could lift it, he tried to move the box. It wasn't really heavy. Maybe a little heavier than the grocery bags he hauled in from the car for his mom each week. He picked up the box and carried it back toward the cave entrance. Maybe I have discovered a pirate's treasure, he thought, excitement bubbling like ginger ale inside him.

He set the box down near the cave entrance where there was enough light to see. "Eric! I found something. It might be a treasure!" he yelled.

No answer. He couldn't see below the ledge, and he didn't want to take time to crawl over to the edge and look over it to see Eric. Maybe Eric didn't hear him. He wouldn't just leave, would he? Ty couldn't worry about it now. He had to see what was in the box before he could leave.

He knelt down in the cave entrance with the box between his knees. He ran his hands, already crusted with dirt, around the edges of the box. There didn't seem to be a lock, just two metal hinges on the back. He put his hands under the lid and pushed up on it. It wouldn't budge. It must have been sealed shut for a very long time, Ty thought. He grabbed for a nearby rock and used it to pound over and over against the top and the sides, all around the box. He threw the rock down and brushed the loosened dirt off the lid of the box, and he saw letters painted on the lid in dark red. "N-I-C-K," it said. Could this Nick be the name of a pirate? He wondered.

Ty heaved again on the lid of the box. This time it moved. He pushed as hard as he could, and slowly the lid creaked open. He tipped it all the way back and, heart pounding, peered inside.

It was so disappointing. No treasure. No shining jewels or glowing golden coins. Not even any paper money. Just a bunch of objects. He reached for them, one at a time, and took them out. Old. That was his first thought. This stuff looked very old. A rusty harmonica. Some nicked-up marbles. A jack knife. A brown leather baseball. A poster. When he unfolded it, Ty saw that the poster advertised a circus. And at the bottom, he found a packet of envelopes tied together with a grubby string. He brought the envelopes closer to his eyes, expecting to see them addressed to someone named Nick.

But they weren't. They were sent to an address in Fayette, but to someone named Loua. A girl's name? Not a name he'd ever heard before, so he couldn't be sure. Could they be from this Nick person? "Only one way to find out," he said aloud.

He opened one of the envelopes and pulled out two pages of handwriting. Scrolling his eyes down to the bottom of the second page, he saw that the signature was "Jimmie." He flipped back to the first page. Ah-ha! The letter began, "Dear Nick and Mama."

These didn't look like the belongings of a pirate. They looked more like things that would belong to a boy. This stuff could have belonged to a boy just like me, who lived in Fayette a long time ago, a boy named Nick, he thought. He closed his eyes for a moment and thought about that. Maybe Mr. Munson was right.

Maybe history really is the stories of interesting people just like us.

Ty opened his eyes and stared off into the distance toward the harbor. He thought he saw a boy sitting on the wooden dock, a long fishing pole held in his hands, feet dangling in the water. But the boy was transparent. Ty could see the grassy bank behind the dock, right through him! He had a quick thought that this was just how Adam had described the people he thought he saw in the hotel. Ty heard something— a voice calling from far away, "Nick! Nick!" The boy on the dock waved an arm.

And for now Ty forgot all about the field trip, Eric, Mr. Munson, and the yellow school bus. He watched the boy on the dock as the figure became clearer and clearer, closer and closer. It was as if he, Ty, were not even there, as if he were absorbed into the boy's life, as if he no longer existed and only the boy was real. He watched the boy, Nick, and his story unfold in his eyes, in his ears, in his head, and in his heart.

Chapter 3
(July, 1881)

Nick sat on the wooden dock, dangling his bare feet into the water of Snail Shell Harbor. He wiggled his feet around in circles, watching the ripples fan out over the sun-sparkled surface. Glancing at the red and white bobber floating at the end of his bamboo fishing pole as it bounced on the ripples, he stopped wiggling his feet. "No use scaring the fish away," he said aloud. He turned to look at the two speckled lake perch lying in the grass behind the dock. One more and he'd have enough to bring home for Mama to fry up for supper. He wrinkled his brow, squinted his eyes, and concentrated on watching the bobber bob.

The sun warmed his face, and the ripples of water hypnotized him. Nick's thoughts floated on the water like his bobber. Fayette, he thought, must be the best place in the world for a boy to live. Nick loved the noise and excitement of the small furnace town. He loved the beaches of Lake Michigan that surrounded it. He loved the swimming, the fishing, the feel of cool water on summer-hot skin. And he loved the people, especially his mama and his friends. He grinned as he thought of his friends and the fun they would have during this special summer of 1881.

Some people complained about the constant noise in the village. But the sounds of Fayette were like music to Nick, filling his ears and his heart with their rhythms. The clanging of machinery from the Jackson Iron Company's blast furnace was as steady as his heartbeat. The din of horses neighing, wagons clattering on rocky roadways and iron ore trains roaring into town were as familiar to him as the sounds of his own breath going in and out. Behind his thoughts, he could hear that music, plus the shouts of children and the squawks of the gulls that constantly soared overhead.

He leaned back and tipped his face up to the warm sun. The whole summer stretched out in front of him. School was out. There was no wood to chop and stack. There was fresh fish for supper and a meeting of his friends' secret club tonight. Life was good, he thought, smiling into the sun.

"Nick!" He heard his name shouted and turned his attention toward town. His best friend Teddy Skidla trotted down the length of the dock toward him. He took his right hand off the fishing pole to wave to Teddy. Just then, a mighty jerk nearly pulled the pole from his left hand. He made a grab, yanking hard on the long shaft of bamboo to hook the fish.

"It's a big one!" he shouted to Teddy as he stood, planting his feet solidly on the boards of the dock. He tried to hoist the long pole out of the water and fling the fish over his head to the grass, but he couldn't. It was just too heavy.

"I see him. I see him!" Teddy shouted, pointing into the water. "He's a lunker."

"Give me a hand!" The pole bent farther into an arch until the tip disappeared under the water. Teddy wrapped his hands around the pole above Nick's.

"On three," Nick directed. "One! Two! Three!" Both boys heaved. The pole snapped up, and a gleaming blue and green speckled fish flew high up out of the water. Their eyes grew wide, and Nick's face split into a huge grin.

Then in one last lunging effort to escape, the fish flopped itself over in mid-air by flipping tail over head. Ping! The fishing line snapped. The pole flew back over their heads. With a huge splash, the fish fell back into the water. It disappeared into the depths. All that was left to be seen were the ripples fanning out in widening circles.

Nick swept the splashed water off his
face with his arm. His shoulders slumped.
He groaned. It was almost enough to make a
grown boy cry.

"That's the biggest fish we ever lost,"
Teddy said. "The guys aren't going to believe it."
He stretched out his hands. "I bet he was
fifteen inches long, and he must have weighed
five pounds."

"Nah!" Nick spread his hands even wider. "I bet he was twenty inches and ten pounds. At least."

"Maybe even twenty-two inches?" The boys looked at each other and laughed.

"Well," Nick admitted, "maybe twelve inches." He bent and picked up his pole, his bucket of worms, and the two smaller fish lying in the grass. "Mama will just have to fry up extra potatoes tonight. Let's go. We've got lots of business to talk about tonight at the club meeting, don't we?"

"Yeah," Teddy agreed. "Like Independence Day coming up and the races and all."

"And the show over at the Music Hall—Professor Loomis's Trained Dog Circus."

"And the problem with your brother Jimmie."

"Yeah, there's always the problem with Jimmie." Nick didn't need reminding.

Teddy nodded solemnly, and the boys walked toward the laborers' log cabins on Cedar Street, south of the village, each lost in his own thoughts, heads down, watchful of where they put their bare feet.

Historic Fayette
Blast Furnace

Chapter 4

Nick was the first to arrive so he chose his favorite spot and leaned against the sun-warmed boards of the back of the livery stable where the club often met. As he waited for the others to arrive, he stared at the long, gray, wooden wagon with its iron wheels that sat beside the barn. He smiled when he thought of how it would look tomorrow. He had a job tomorrow. That job was mucking out the livery stable, shoveling the horse manure and dirty straw onto the wagon to be hauled away from town. A paid job.

While he chewed on the skin around his thumbnail, he thought about what he could do with the money he was saving from doing odd jobs this summer. Tickets to Professor Loomis's Trained Dog Circus cost 35 cents. The silver-plated harmonica he'd seen at the company store was $1.50. Fishing hooks and bobbers were 5 cents each. The chewy, buttery caramel candies he loved sold for two for a penny.

Colored glass cat's-eye marbles were 2 for 5 cents. A baseball cost 40 cents, and a bat was worth 65 cents. Nick was good at numbers, and he added them up in his head. The total was high, impossibly high. If he had a job every day for a whole year, he probably would not have enough money for all the things he wanted. But tomorrow, thanks to the constant supply of manure the horses created, he'd add to the coins he kept hidden, knotted in the toe of a big winter wool sock.

"I, Archibald Talbot, president, call this meeting of the club to order."

Nick looked at Teddy across the circle, and Teddy rolled his eyes.

"Everyone stand for the pledge," Archie ordered. Six boys rose from the grass and stood. They each spit into the palms of their left hands and rubbed two hands together fast. Then they placed their right palms over their hearts and repeated the secret pledge.

"We pledge our loyalty to the club and promise to solve mysteries and do deeds that need to be done. Criss-cross our hearts and hope to die; we will only share our secrets with the sky."

The boys made X's on their chests and then plunked down again to sprawl on the grass in a circle with their bare feet pointing toward each other.

"First item of business," Archie continued, "is solving mysteries." He spread his gaze around the circle of boys. "Any news? Anything mysterious need to be solved?"

Joe Bayfield spoke up. "Well, there's always the case of the missing treasure. We've been working on that one ever since the ice was off the harbor last spring." He shrugged his shoulders. "Nothing new to report."

The boys all looked glum. In the spring they had been so confident that they could solve the mystery and find the treasure. But after months of searching the dolomite caves along the harbor and digging tons of sand and rocks with shovels and picks and bare fingers, they were discouraged.

"I'm beginning to think there is no treasure. Someone probably just made up the whole thing as a joke or as a way to get visitors to come to Fayette. You know, treasure hunters," Tom McNally said.

Tom's twin, Mike, disagreed. "No. I think it's real. Look at the facts." He began to number them on his fingers. "First, we know that the company doesn't allow any drinking of alcohol in Fayette. Alcohol is against the law. But we also know that people been drinking it anyhow. Right?"

The boys nodded. They knew what they'd seen and heard around town. Since their job was solving mysteries and doing deeds that needed to be done, they always had to be alert and observant of what was happening around town.

"Second," Mike held up another finger, "we know that they got their whiskey from Alphonse Berlanguette at his illegal shack down the beach. That is, until he ran off and the township committee went and burned it down. But Berlanguette had plenty of time to get the safe with his money out of there and hide his treasure. Unfortunately, he died suddenly, before he could tell anyone else where he hid it."

Heads nodded around the circle.

"I know my stepfather alone drinks enough whiskey to make Berlanguette a rich man," Nick admitted with disgust, trying not to think about some of the things his stepfather, Frank Demone, said and did, especially to Jimmie, when he'd had too much to drink.

"I can't think of anything else we can do," Archie said. "Unless we get more clues, we probably have to put the case of the missing treasure in our unsolved mysteries file."

Teddy rolled his eyes at Nick again. As if they had files. The only files the club had were inside Archie's head, along with a lot of other strange and highfalutin notions. The others thought Archie read too many books and got too many big ideas. Sometimes he couldn't remember what was real and what was in books.

"Next item of business, Professor Loomis's Trained Dog Circus." The boys around the circle perked up. They had been looking forward to this show for weeks. Every two weeks there was some sort of entertainment or traveling act at the Music Hall. So far all summer, there hadn't been much to interest them. There'd been an actress, a couple of concerts by the Fayette Coronet Band, a fiery preacher, and a women's rights speaker. The only interesting act was a minstrel band of all black men. The boys hadn't gone to the concert. Twenty-five cents for a ticket was a big chunk of money to them. But still they had hung around outside the back steps of the Music Hall so they could see the black-faced performers up close. Most of the boys had never seen a black person before, so they were intrigued. They discovered that these musicians were friendly and just like most of the other nice people who passed through town.

But now, finally, came a show to interest them. They'd all been trying to earn money doing odd jobs around town so they could see the dog circus.

"Does everybody have the twenty-five cents for a ticket?" Archie asked.

Nick nodded, even though he wouldn't have the last nickel until after he worked tomorrow. The other boys nodded, except for the twins, Tom and Mike. All eyes turned to them.

"We only got forty cents all together," Tom admitted. "Maybe we'll have to flip a coin and only one of us go."

"Nah," Nick said. "I will have ten cents extra. You can have it. We all gotta go."

"Gee, thanks, Nick," a smiling Mike said. "We'll owe you." Both twins had big grins on their faces. Just looking at them made Nick feel glad that he'd helped.

Nick smiled back. "Sure." He knew he'd probably never get paid back. The McNally family had too many mouths to feed. Mr. McNally had one of the lowest jobs at the furnace, and Mrs. McNally was so busy and worn out from taking care of seven children that she couldn't bake or take in laundry or roomers or any of the other things some families did to earn extra money.

Oh, well, Nick thought. It would just mean giving up eating caramel candies for a while. He could live with that easier than having one of the twins miss the dog circus.

"We'll meet here at six thirty and go together so we can get good seats up front," Archie announced. "Next business— Independence Day is just a few days away. Now, there are deeds that need doing for that."

"What do we need to do?" Joe asked.
Joe was a newcomer to Fayette; he hadn't been
there last July Fourth for the town's celebration.
All the boys in the circle began telling him
about Fayette's Independence Day, the best day
in the whole year.

"First, there's the parade," Teddy said.

"There's the horse races. Fayette's fastest
horses against the fastest they have from the
village of Garden," Mike added.

"And the baseball game. Fayette against
Garden," said Tom.

"And all kinds of races and contests,"
Nick put in.

"Especially the Fat Man Race," Archie
explained. The boys laughed as each
remembered the biggest men in the village
racing down the track in their underwear. They
began to shout, their voices tumbling over each
other's as they added details to their story of
the Fourth of July.

"And a potluck supper with the best and
the most food you ever saw."

"And a dance."

"And, then, best of all, the fireworks over
the harbor."

"It sounds great," Joe said, his eyes
lighting up with each new activity he heard
about.

"It is," the boys promised in unison.

"And this year there's a surprise—
Jimmie's act," Nick said.

The boys turned toward him. He felt a
sinking feeling in his stomach. His brother
Jimmie's act. The danger. The excitement.
And what it would mean to his family if Jimmie
were successful, or unsuccessful, that day.
The sinking feeling in his stomach turned into
a knot. Independence Day was coming soon,
too soon. His life would change that day.
He brought his fist up to his mouth and chewed
on his thumbnail.

Chapter 5

"What are the deeds that need doing for Independence Day?" Joe asked.

"We've got to decorate my velocipede," Archie said. "I've got red, white, and blue crepe paper to weave through the spokes of both wheels and streamers to tie on the handlebars. My mother's even making me an Uncle Sam suit out of some old clothes and sheets. I've got to try to win the decorating contest. The prize is fifty cents. We've got to decide who is going to be in what races. Selling the drinks and food at the baseball game is a good money-maker. We get to keep a penny for each one we sell. And, of course, there's the problem of figuring out what to do about Jimmie."

"Is his act any good? Has anybody besides Nick seen him practicing?" asked Joe.

"I have," Teddy said. "He's got a rope strung up between two trees (higher than me) out in the woods." The boys laughed. Teddy was the shortest boy in the group. The top of his head only came up to Nick's chin. Teddy ignored them. "Every day he goes out there and he balances and does tricks on that rope. To my mind, he's just as good as the tightrope walker that was in the Sells Brothers' Circus that came to Escanaba."

"That's where he got the idea," Nick explained. "When he saw the Sells Brothers' tightrope walker, it was like a spell came over him. He was bound and determined that he was going to learn how to walk the tightrope himself and run off and join the circus. Jimmie's always wanted to get away from Fayette and the furnace and see the big, wide world."

The boys all knew that one reason Jimmie wanted to get away was Frank Demone, his and Nick's stepfather. Frank pretty much ignored Nick, for which he was thankful. But, for some reason, all their stepfather's anger, all his bitterness and ornery meanness were directed at Jimmie. He'd been their stepfather for four years now, three years of which Jimmie had suffered from cruel words and harsh blows to his body.

For the thousandth time, Nick wished his real father had not died in the accident at the furnace and that his mother had never remarried. He could understand why she had, but he still wished she hadn't, at least not to Demone.

After his father had died, burned in a
fiery accident, his mama had tried to make it
on her own, taking care of her two sons. She
took in laundry; she cooked meals for single
men who worked in the furnace or the forest.
Jimmie tried to help. He quit school and
worked. But he was only twelve and couldn't
earn much running errands, chopping wood,
and shoveling snow. They got poorer and poorer
until Mama just didn't know how they were
going to keep together, let alone keep warm
and healthy during the long, cold winter. Then
Frank Demone offered marriage, a warm cabin,
a steady income from the blast furnace, and a
second chance for her family. Mama took it.

They moved into Frank's cabin. At first,
everything seemed better. Mama wasn't so tired.
The lines in her face smoothed out. They had
enough food to eat, clothes to wear, and wood
to keep warm. Two babies came in the next
three years, both girls. Frank made it plain he
didn't have much use for girls. "What good are
they?" he said. "How could they ever help
support the family?" And the family was
needing more and more support, especially as
Frank drank more and more whiskey.

When he drank whiskey, Frank got mean.
He said hateful things to Mama. But mostly,
he vented his anger on Jimmie. Sweet-natured,
fragile-looking Jimmie, who loved to read and

got good conduct ribbons at school, was his favorite target. Jimmie was not Frank's idea of a brawny lad to be proud to call his son. Pansy. Weakling. Little girlie. Pantywaist. Those were some of the names he called Jimmie. Jimmie took it, the name calling and eventually the beatings, without ever saying a word. But he lived for the day he could get away. He'd been planning for months, ever since he had gone to Escanaba on the boat and had seen the Sells Brothers' Circus.

And now his chance was coming soon—on Independence Day. Independence Day, Nick thought, was just what the Fourth of July would be for Jimmie, if all went according to their plans.

Nick and Jimmie had been sleeping outside all summer, unless it was raining. They brought their pillows and a blanket to the beach and slept under the stars, thankful for the wide, open space and the cool breezes rather than the hot, stuffy cabin loft where the whole family slept.

Late into the nights they lay, wrapped in their blankets, snuggled down into the soft beach sand, staring at the star-filled sky, talking and planning. Jimmie didn't cough in the night when they slept in the open air. "It's from the smoke at the furnace," he'd explained to Nick. "Gets stuck in my lungs sometimes,

36

I think. I hate the furnace. I hate the noise that makes my head ache and the heat and the smoke that make me cough. I can't wait to get out of there. If I had to spend my whole life working there, I might as well be dead."

And now Jimmie was going to get his chance to get away from the furnace and their stepfather. He was going to do his tightrope-walking act, although he called it an exhibition, for the whole village of Fayette at the Independence Day celebration. If it went well, if the crowd liked his act, then the boys in the club were going to take up a collection to help him go off to join the circus. One night he had confided in Nick that he'd met the ropewalker at the Sells Brothers' Circus and that they'd talked about how he could learn to walk the tightrope. The walker, an older man named Johnny Crabb, had been kind and generous. He had given Jimmie advice and tips and showed him how to get started. He told Jimmie it was a God-given gift, the talent he had, one that very few people in the whole world possessed. Told Jimmie how to practice. Told him that he was planning to retire from the circus in the coming year and if Jimmie got good at it, he might be able to take his place. They'd been corresponding. Jimmie showed Nick the last letter he'd gotten. In it, Crabb said he'd had an accident, had fallen from the rope and hurt his back. He was ready to quit. Did Jimmie think he was ready to come and show the Sells Brothers what he could do? He included the circus's schedule, what towns they would be in and when. The week after Independence Day, the circus would be in Rhinelander, Wisconsin. It was the closest the circus would get to Fayette this summer. Jimmie was going to go. All he needed was the self-confidence he'd get if the town said his act was good enough and the money for a train ticket and some food.

Although mostly Nick was glad for Jimmie, part of him was sad for himself. He was sure going to miss his big brother. And he couldn't help but wonder what Frank's reaction would be. Would he be glad that Jimmie was gone out of his life and cabin? Would he be happy to have one less mouth to feed? Or would he be angry? Would he miss having Jimmie's wages? Would he miss having Jimmie to pick on? And, Nick couldn't help but worry, would he need to find someone else to abuse? And, if so, who would the someone else be? Him? Mama? The little girls? It was something to worry about.

Chapter 6

"So, let's say Jimmie's act is good. The town loves him. We've got to pass the hat and take up the collection right away," said Archie.

"But first we have to make some kind of announcement so the crowd knows we're collecting for Jimmie," Nick added.

"I could ask my father to make an announcement," Archie volunteered.

"No," Nick said. "We've got to keep it a secret right up until the last possible minute. Even my mother can't know ahead."

"Yeah," Teddy agreed. "If Demone found out, he could try to stop him."

The boys were silent, thinking. Finally, Teddy said, "I think I know how to make the announcement. Leave it to me. I'll figure it out. Don't worry." He smiled, and his friends seemed to believe him.

The boys all nodded solemnly. There was a little more discussion of the plan. Who was going to cover which section of the crowd?

How would they meet up with Jimmie and give him the money? Would he be able to catch a ride on the boat with the Garden village baseball team and then go on to Escanaba to the train and be off to join the Sells Brothers' Circus? Nick knew he wouldn't breathe easy until Jimmie was far out of his stepfather's reach. And maybe not even then, he thought, as a cold shiver ran up his spine. He bit down again on his thumbnail.

"Now I got big news," Archie said, sounding his most important self. "You all know my dad; he's got a high job at the furnace."

Of course they all knew that. Archie reminded them every chance he got that his father was a shift foreman. It wasn't really high up on the ladder of importance at the furnace, not a management-type job, but it was higher up than the common laborer jobs their fathers held. And they all knew that the money, the prestige, the kind and amount of work a man did depended on how high up the ladder his job with the company put him. The dirtiest, hardest jobs went to those on the bottom rungs of the social ladder, the common laborers, the pig iron handlers, the colliers who worked the charcoal kilns.

"So?" Tom asked after a moment of silence, waiting for Archie to share his big news. "What is it, Arch?"

"Well," said Archie, drawing out his suspense. "The company's got a professional photographer coming to take pictures of the furnace operation and all the workers. And my dad says, since we help out sometimes, running errands and sweeping, and such, we can be in the photograph, too."

"Geez," said Mike. "I never had my picture took before."

"Me either," all of the boys chorused.

"It's tomorrow," said Archie. "We got to be outside, in front of the furnace, and ready when the noon whistle blows."

That was going to take some doing, Nick thought. He'd be working here at the stable, shoveling the muck out of the stalls and loading it onto the wagon. He'd have to work hard all morning, trying to stay as clean as possible for the photograph. He would eat his bread and cheese lunch while he ran over to the furnace. They'd get the picture taken, and then he would run back and shovel like crazy to get the stable cleaned out before the wagon left at 3:00.

"Boy, ain't this going to be the most exciting week of our lives?" said Teddy. All the boys grinned and nodded, thinking of the photograph, the dog show, the Independence Day celebrations, and Jimmie's exhibition and escape. Nick reached his fingers down and bent two toes on each foot so they crossed. Then he crossed all the fingers on both his hands. He squeezed his eyes together, making a wish that, by the end of the week, they'd all be happy—especially Jimmie.

"Meeting adjourned," Archie announced.

Chapter 7

When the whistle blew at noon the next day, Nick was already trotting toward the furnace. He'd worked hard, shoveling out the stable, sweating and straining since first light. Fifteen minutes earlier he'd headed for the pump, splashing water on his face and neck, running wet fingers through his hair, which he didn't have much of since his summer haircut. Rolling up the cuffs of his pants, he let the icy water flow over his legs and feet. He scrubbed on them, paying particular attention to the front of his legs and tops of his feet, which would show in the photograph. He dried his hands on his pants and fished his bread and cheese sandwich out of his pocket. He stretched his mouth open as far as it would go, took a huge bite, and chewed as he ran toward the furnace.

As he approached, he could see the furnace workers gathering. And there was the photographer, about ten yards in front of the furnace, dressed like a city man in a brown suit with a long coat and a sparkling, clean, white shirt. He was unpacking two wooden boxes as Nick came near. In one box Nick could see the big, square, black and silver camera. In the other box, glass plates, like small, thick windows, stood in a row.

"Good day," he said, remembering his manners.

The photographer looked up at Nick and smiled. "Nice day for a photograph," he said. "Not too sunny. Won't have too many harsh shadows. Men won't be squinting." He looked up at the gray, overcast sky above Fayette. "Yup, perfect day for photography."

"I'm going to be in the photo," Nick announced proudly.

The photographer didn't reply, just continued his work of unpacking and setting up for the shot. Nick was interested in the equipment. He'd never seen a camera before and was curious about how images could be captured on glass windows and tin plates. It seemed like a miracle to him. He watched as the photographer set up a wooden tripod and carefully lifted the boxy camera. He placed it on a little platform atop the tripod and turned a wooden screw to secure it there.

So engrossed was he with the photography equipment that at first he didn't hear Archie shouting his name. "Nick! Nick! Get over here." He turned reluctantly from the tripod and box of glass plates and walked to where Archie stood in front of the men who were lining up.

Two rows of men stood on the ground. They were the pig iron handlers and other common laborers. He saw Frank in the front row, on the left, posing with left leg extended and right hand on his hip, looking cocky, sure of himself, darkly handsome. A few men, elevated on crates and stacks of wood, stood behind the first rows. Others were higher yet. A row of men balanced on one of the large pipes running out of the furnace. Archie's father was among them. Another row of about ten men stood on the narrow ledge a third of the way up the brick side of the furnace building. They must be the shift bosses, he thought. A few men perched on ladders, and way up on the roof, standing proudly, was J.B. Kitchen, the furnace superintendent, dressed in work clothes today, not office clothes, for the photo. Funny, Nick thought. He wondered if the men had been given orders to line up for the photo in descending order, showing their rank in the company, or if it had just happened that way without thought. And here we are, down front, the least important of all, the boys.

46

The photographer shouted to get attention. "Gentlemen. We are just about ready to take the photograph. Be sure you are in position. Soon I will ask you to remain absolutely still while the image is exposed. I will count down from five. At zero, I will take the image. It is important that you do not move for a full sixty seconds. Do not move a muscle until I tell you."

Nick glanced at the boys lining up beside him. He and Teddy grinned at each other. Archie tried to look important. A younger boy had joined them. Somebody's little brother, maybe one of the McNally kids, he thought. On the end of their row, an older boy, Eugene Colwell, all dressed up like he was going to church on Easter morning, stood ramrod straight. "But where are the others from the club?" he asked Archie.

"Don't know about Joe. But Tom and Mike had to go out to the sawmill where their father is and take him his lunch. He's at a new mill they started, deeper into the forest and farther away from Fayette. He has to stay at the kiln for eight days, until the batch of charcoal is ready. That's the way it is for colliers."

"Too bad," Nick said.

"Why?" The voice came from above his left shoulder. He looked up into the scowling face of Eugene Colwell. "Who needs more barefoot boys? It will be an embarrassment to the company." He looked pointedly down at the feet of Nick, Archie, Teddy, and the other boy. Nick dropped his eyes and saw that Eugene had on socks and brown, lace-up shoes.

"What do shoes have to do with anything?" he asked Eugene. "Hardly anyone wears shoes in the summer."

"Hardly anyone of the lower class," Eugene amended, looking down his nose at Nick and laughing at his own cleverness.

Nick felt shame creeping like maroon wool up his neck and over his cheeks. He dropped his gaze to his own dusty, bare feet. He closed his eyes and pretended that his mother was stitching his lips together with embroidery thread so he couldn't open them and yell, "Shut up!"

Then he heard Archie's calm voice. "Goes to show how ignorant you are," said Archie slowly and loudly. "You don't even know about the Secret Barefoot Boys Society. They wouldn't have you for a member."

"What secret society?" Eugene asked.

"Well, if I told you, it wouldn't be a secret society any more, would it?"

"So, how do you get in it?" Eugene was curious despite himself.

"You've got to be worthy," Archie proclaimed in his most dramatic voice, leaving no doubt that Eugene would not be considered worthy.

Archie amazed Nick. Suddenly, he understood why Archie was always chosen as the leader. Even at school, he was always elected class president. Archie could think fast and creatively. He could get people to believe, to follow. He inspired confidence. Nick guessed those things all added up to leadership. Archie had leadership. And on top of all that, Archie always stood up for his friends. Nick gave him a secret smile while Eugene Colwell blew a breath out in frustration.

"Five.......four......three......"

Nick adjusted himself, planted his bare feet firmly in the dirt, pushed his shoulders back to look tall, gripped tightly on the cap he held in front of him with both hands, and got ready to smile.

"Two.......one.........zero. Stop! Don't move." The photographer, his head under a black cloth at the back of the camera, slid the glass plate out of the camera. "Steady. Steady. Don't move. Don't move. That's it."

Nick's nose began to tickle. He wanted to reach up and scratch it, and he almost did. Just as he started to move his hand up, he heard the photographer's voice again. "Steady. Steady. Almost done. Good. There. You can breathe again."

Nick could feel the collected breaths of all the furnace workers exhaled on the back of his neck. The photographer came out from under his black cover, turned the glass plate around, and inserted it back into the camera. "Let's try that one more time, just to be sure we got it." Nick reached up and scratched his nose before they had to stay still again. "Ready?" the photographer asked.

"Five.....four.....three.....two......one....zero."

It was only after the final shot was taken that Nick remembered his lips were still stitched together. He swiped the back of his hand across his mouth. Oh, well, he sighed. It will just be a closed-mouth smile in the photograph, he told himself. Eugene Colwell walked off, and Nick turned to Archie. "That was great, what you told him."

"It's the truth," Archie said, laughing. "From now on, we'll be The Secret Barefoot Boys Society. It's a great name, don't you think?"

Nick and Teddy agreed. Nick waved at his friends and hurried off toward the stable to finish his job and collect his pay.

Chapter 8

The Barefoot Boys Secret Society met at the Music Hall entrance. They were early, arriving long before the doors were scheduled to open, so they could get front row seats and a clear view of all the dog tricks they expected to see. Nick handed Tom and Mike two nickels so they could buy their tickets. "Thanks," they said, showering Nick with identical toothy grins. It gave him a good feeling to help his friends.

Nick looked up at the second story of the wooden building, one of the largest buildings in Fayette, besides the furnace and the hotel, of course. The first floor contained the village barber, the butcher, and the granary. Upstairs was a large, open space with a raised stage at one end. Wooden benches stood in rows on either side of a center aisle.

Nick's insides were feeling all jumpy and excited. He'd been waiting for weeks to see Professor Loomis's Trained Dog Circus. Finally, it was here. But as he looked upward at the top

51

floor, the Music Hall floor, a weird and fearful feeling washed over him. Then he realized why. He remembered last spring, the last time he had been in the Music Hall. The humiliation. He shivered so hard that Teddy, standing beside him, noticed.

"You cold?" Teddy asked.

"Nah." Nick shrugged, trying to shake off the feeling. "I get the heebie-jeebie creepy crawlies up my back just thinking about going into the Music Hall again, the scene of my spelling bee disaster," he admitted.

"So you lost. It wasn't really a disaster. After all, you got farther than any of the rest of us," Teddy assured him.

But to Nick it was a disaster. The scene of the spelling bee replayed across his mind. He could see his mother and Jimmie in the audience, smiling proudly as he represented Fayette's fifth grade against the best spellers from the Garden school. Actually, truth to tell, he knew he shouldn't even have been the fifth-grade champion. Loua Bellows should have won the honor. But she was sick that week, and by some strange trick of fate he'd outspelled the others. How could it happen that he got all the words he knew? It was a deep, dark mystery to him. Now that was a mystery the club could never solve, he thought.

Soon he was the only one left standing

and was declared the Fayette School fifth-grade spelling champion. That meant that he would represent his school and his town in the annual competition between the best spellers of Fayette and Garden. The two schools, the two towns, were always finding something to have a contest about. And Fayette's honor was at stake more than usual this year because the weekly newspaper from Escanaba had printed a story that made Fayette School and its students look bad. The children were "ignorant," the newspaper said. They didn't know anything about the governor of the great state of Michigan. When a touring representative from the capitol in Lansing had asked them who the governor was, they "had replied with united voices, 'Fayette Brown.'" They were wrong about Michigan. Everyone should know the governor was David H. Jerome. But "they only knew who was 'boss' in their town," the article concluded.

Fayette Brown was the agent and manager of the Jackson Iron Company which had started the furnace at Fayette. He had picked the site at Fayette because there seemed to be an unlimited supply of hardwood trees for making charcoal. It had limestone cliffs for building and for making the flux needed in the smelting process. And there was the beautiful Snail Shell Harbor so boats could come and go on Great Lakes shipping routes. The mining company named the town after Fayette Brown. He visited the town several times each year. So it was only natural that the children would know and respect his name. The people of Fayette were angry that their school and students had been called ignorant in the newspaper.

So the town's honor, as well as that of the school and its students, was at stake. Nick felt the weight of the responsibility on his shoulders, and he took it seriously. He would be the one to salvage the town's honor and reputation. He would make the town proud. He began to study the words every night. Jimmie quizzed him on them. He felt nervous, but he was ready when the big night came.

There sat his mother and Jimmie smiling proudly. Almost the whole town and half of Garden, it seemed to him, had crowded into the upstairs Music Hall. It was heating up. Nick felt sweat gather and trickle down his neck. His hands were sweaty, too. He'd bet that, if he took his stockings and school shoes off, his feet would be sweaty, too.

They did the younger kids first, starting with the third graders and then the fourth graders. His nervousness grew as he waited for them to finish. It took forever. They went back and forth, back and forth, about twenty words each, he estimated. When it came time for the fifth grade, Fayette had won one ribbon; Garden had won one. Now it was time for the fifth-grade champions to go head-to-head. Nellie LaFontaine was the name of the girl representing Garden School. She looked smart and confident, Nick thought. He squared his shoulders and tried to look confident, too.

Nellie spelled her first word, *article* correctly. Nick's word was *bounce*. He took a deep breath and his voice hardly squeaked as he spelled it, "Bounce. B-o-u-n-c-e. Bounce."

"Correct."

Nellie LaFontaine spelled her next word, *business,* correctly. Nick got his second word, *opportunity*. His mind went blank. Opportunity? Oh, my gosh. Is it one *p* or two? Is it *er* or *or*? At the end, is it two *t*'s or one? His brain turned to ice, a big chunk of ice with the word *opportunity* trapped inside. He scrunched up his eyes, trying, but he couldn't see the word. Fractures in the ice. Fractures in his brain.

The announcer repeated the word. "Opportunity."

Nick took a big breath. He had to begin. There was a time limit. "Opportunity. O-p-p-o-r-t-u-n- ...." He breathed in again and then squirted the ending of the word out, "i-t-t-y, opportunity," on a big exhaled breath.

"That is incorrect," said the announcer. Nick's heart dropped. "For the win, Miss LaFontaine, spell *opportunity*."

55

Nick glanced at Nellie, and he could tell by her nod and her smile that she knew how to spell the word. And suddenly he did, too. It only had one *t* at the end. "Stupid. Stupid. Stupid," he told himself as Nellie LaFontaine won the spelling bee on the second word. The second word! There was nothing his mother or Jimmie could be proud of now. He felt as low as a toad's belly. Head hanging, he made his slow-stepped, loser way across the stage.

Now, waiting to go into the Music Hall, the scene of his public humiliation, Nick tried to shake off the memories. Think about the dogs, he told himself, about Professor Loomis's Dog Circus. Someday he would have a dog of his own, and it would love only him. He would teach it tricks, and maybe he would name it Opportunity and call it Op for short. He laughed at the thought, just as the doors to the Music Hall opened.

Chapter 9

"C'mon. Let's get the front row." That was important to Teddy. Being so short, he would have a hard time seeing over the heads of people in front of him. He grabbed Nick's arm, and the boys pushed up to the doorway and handed the ticket seller their coins. The ticket seller was a large woman with mounds of reddish hair piled high on her head, eyes outlined in black, with bright, red lips stretched over long yellowed teeth. She took their coins into her hand just before they disappeared into the folds of her long, black cape. The other hand, covered with rings, gave them each a paper ticket. "Enjoy zee show, boys," she said in a strange accent.

Halfway up the stairs to the Music Hall, Teddy stopped and turned around. "Eeen-zoy zee shooo, bo-eeze," he said, fluttering his eyelashes and smiling so all his teeth showed.

The boys laughed. Nick was always amazed at Teddy's talent for mimicking people.

Sometimes, if Nick wasn't looking right at him, he would swear it was furnace superintendent J.B. Kitchen or Doc Bellows or Mr. Pinchin from the store talking. Teddy could even do girls, which angered them in the schoolyard, but made all the boys laugh.

"Ah, we should have known," Archie said, shaking his head at the ribbon stretched across the first row of benches. "Reserved," the sign said. "Probably reserved for J.B. Kitchen and his family." The boys shrugged and settled on the second row bench on the left side of the center aisle to wait impatiently for the hall to fill and the dog circus to begin.

Soon the benches were full, including the first row with furnace superintendent Mr. Kitchen and his family and friends. From the right side of the stage, an incredible sight appeared. It was a woman with piles of curly red hair on top of her head. Tall, yellow feathers danced on top of the curls as she stepped forward and made a bow. She stood, wrapped in a yellow satin cape, waiting for the crowd to quiet.

"Ladeeeze and gentlemen," she announced loudly in her strange accent, "in one leeetle moment you will have zee great pleasure of seeing zee astounding Professor Loomiz and hees amazing dogs which he has trained himself for many years."

60

She swept her arms out, spreading the cape like bat wings, and then flipped it over the shoulders of a black gown glittering with sequins and beads. She walked majestically down the three steps to the piano at the right side of the hall and seated herself with a flourish.

"Zeeee show begins!" She pounded her ringed fingers on the piano keys. A French can-can song filled the Music Hall as Professor Loomis appeared on stage in a black tuxedo with long tails flapping to his knees in back and a tall, black top hat perched on his head. Under his hat, the thing Nick noticed most was the shiny black mustache that curled into a circle on each cheek. He paraded across the stage to the music and was followed by five small dogs that were dressed in ruffled can-can skirts and that were wearing feathered headdresses much like the lady's. Turning in circles across the stage, the dogs danced on their hind legs.

The crowd clapped and yelled. "Oooh, la, la!" someone called.

When they reached the other side of the stage, the Professor gave each dog a treat as they fell to all four feet. That must be how he trains them, Nick thought. He gave Teddy a nudge. "I wonder how long it took to teach them all to do that!"

And that was only the opening act. Next came a mama dog, dressed in an apron, walking on her back legs and pushing a baby dog in a carriage. The dog playing the baby wore a lacy bonnet. The crowd went wild when the baby jumped out of the carriage and ran around it in circles wearing a diaper over its back end.

The Professor set up two little sets of steps with a narrow, wooden plank stretched between them. One dog ran up the steps and walked slowly and carefully across the narrow plank to the other set of steps. It reminded Nick of Jimmie's rope-walking exhibition.

One dog did back flips—three in a row. Another dog bounced a large ball up in the air using his nose. A third dog balanced on top of a big ball and walked, rolling the ball under him and keeping his balance, until he reached the other side of the stage. Then the Professor took the plank down and pushed the steps nearer each other. He stood between them. The red-haired lady pounded out a Sousa march on the piano as the Professor held up a hoop and each dog ran up the steps, leaped through the hoop, and ran down the other steps.

The music stopped, and the Professor took a bow. He pointed to the dogs, all lined up, and they stretched out their front legs, put their heads down, and wagged their tails in the air for their bow. They trotted off the stage.

The crowd cheered and cheered. The boys stood up, clapping and stomping their feet. "Encore!" someone yelled, and the crowd took up the chant until the Professor came back on stage. The lady joined him, and they both bowed. "Encore!" the chant continued.

The lady raised her arms, then lowered them, and began to speak. The crowd hushed. "Thank you, ladeeeze and gentlemen. You are most kind. Because of thees, the Professor will honor you weeth a trick that has never before been attempted in Northern Michigan. Zee fire hoop!"

A buzz went through the crowd. She strode to one side of the stage and emerged with a hoop wrapped in cloth and a candle. The Professor went backstage and emerged with a small black and white dog in his arms. He set the dog down at the left steps, took the hoop from the lady, and put it in the grips of a long-handled grabbing tool, like the ones loggers and colliers used to hold tree limbs and pieces of charcoal. The lady touched the candle to the hoop, and flames began spreading around it.

"Oooooooh!" came the in-drawn breaths of the crowd. Nick looked from the fire to the dog as it stood still at the side of the stage. He was a small dog, nearly all black, except for white on each paw, like socks, and a white tip on his tail. To Nick, he looked, like a black dog

63

that had stepped into a tray of white paint.

Standing in his spot between the sets of steps, the Professor called the dog. It did not move. He called again. Still the dog did not move. The crowd began to murmur. The flames surrounded the perimeter of the hoop now. The Professor's face grew red. From heat or anger, Nick did not know. The Professor barked out a command, sharper this time, and slapped his leg. Suddenly, the little dog jumped into action. It bounded up the stairs, leaped into the air, and headed for the flaming hoop. Nick held his breath.

The dog sailed on, a black and white blur, through the yellow and orange flames and landed on the opposite steps. Nick let out his breath in a long sigh of relief.

The crowd cheered and hollered. The Professor scooped up the dog, grabbed the lady's hand, and they bowed one last time.

Nick clapped until his hands were stinging. But he kept thinking about what could have happened if the little dog had not jumped cleanly through the middle of the circle of fire.

Chapter 10

"That was some show," said Teddy.

"Worth every penny," Archie agreed.

The boys tumbled down the stairs, through the doorway, and out into a balmy summer evening. Glad to be running after sitting on hard benches for so long, they dodged through the crowd as they chased each other.

Just in front of him, Archie stopped so suddenly that Nick ran into him. "Look!" he whispered to Nick with an indrawn breath. "Over by the side of the butcher's shop. See him? It's Tanny-bum!"

"No foolin'?"

"Gotta be. See the long overcoat with the cap pulled low, and the long gray beard, and the gunny sack he's carrying? It's Tanny-bum, all right."

Teddy, Joe, and the McNally twins had come up beside Nick and Archie and heard.

"Who's he?" asked Joe, the newcomer.

"He's .....he's Tanny-bum. He's weird and scary. He doesn't talk," began Mike.

His twin, Tom, continued, "See that sack? They say he steals little kids and puts them in his sack and runs off with them, and they are never heard from again!"

"Let's get out of here before he sees us," Teddy suggested urgently.

The boys took off as fast as they could run, up the road toward Doc Bellows's and J.B. Kitchen's houses, as far away as they could get from the Music Hall and the scary figure of Tanny-bum.

Chests heaving and sides aching, they stopped at a rock outcropping not far from the doctor's house. They were all breathing too hard to talk at first. Finally, Teddy caught his breath and asked, "Do you think he saw us?"

"Nah. We got away fast," Archie assured his friends. "But if Tanny-bum is here in Fayette, we'd better look out. I hope he'll be gone by July Fourth."

"Is his name really Tanny-bum?" asked Joe.

Archie, of course, knew the answer. "No. His name is Tannenbaum." He pronounced it slowly. "Tan- en-bomb. I think it's a German name."

"I don't know about German," Teddy added, "but I know crazy, and he's it."

Joe still had a perplexed look on his face. Archie filled in the rest of the information. "When little Loua Bellows first came to live with her grandma and grandpa, Doc Bellows, we were talking about Tannenbaum and how he buys and sells rags and junk, and travels around, and makes grunty noises but doesn't talk, and how he probably uses that sack to steal little kids. Loua got scared and started blabbering, 'Tanny-bum won't ever catch me!' It was kind of funny, because it sounded like Tiny-bum, and he doesn't have a tiny bum." The boys laughed at the familiar joke. "Pretty soon all the kids were calling him Tanny-bum." Archie shrugged.

"They say he tells folks in Garden that he lives in Fayette," said Mike.

"But he tells people in Fayette that he lives in Garden," added Tom.

"No one knows where he lives. When he's here, he never stays at the hotel like other visitors. I think he sleeps in the woods. When he goes to people's houses, they feed him and give him stuff so he won't steal their kids," Teddy said. Nick remembered Frank Demone threatening the little girls that if they didn't behave Tanny-bum would take them away in his sack.

Dusk was settling over Fayette when Archie said, "Look who's coming." He pointed down the road where they had come. Nick was almost afraid to look, thinking it was Tanny-bum. But it was Loua Bellows and Jenny Marchant, walking arm-in-arm toward home. They stopped at the corner, and Jenny turned off toward her house. The boys heard the two girls shouting "Good bye" over and over again as they got farther apart.

Teddy rolled his eyes. "Girls," he mumbled.

"Aw, Loua's not bad," Nick said, and then felt a flush rush into his cheeks as his friends laughed at him.

"You sweet on her?" Mike asked. Nick shook his head vehemently.

"Hey, Loua, did you see Tanny-bum?" Archie asked as she approached. "He's here in Fayette. Probably looking for little girls to stuff in his sack and carry off." He had made his voice sound low and spooky.

"Tanny-bum? He's here?" Loua clutched her arms across her chest as if suddenly chilled.

All the boys nodded.

"Oh, I wish Jenny had come home with me ...."

"Why? You scared to walk home alone?" Joe asked.

"Me? Scared? 'Course not. But, maybe Jenny is." She looked over her shoulder at the darkening road that was overhung with trees.

"I'll walk the rest of the way with you,"

70

Nick volunteered.

The boys jabbed at each other and made googly eyes.

"Jimmie wanted me to talk to her about something," he tried to explain to his friends as they got up from the rocks and headed down the road.

"Yah, sure."

"Ah-huh. Right."

"Whatever you say."

Loua took a few steps toward her house, and Nick caught up with her. "It's sweet of you to walk me home," she said.

"Well, ah, Jimmie did want me to ask you about something."

"Your brother Jimmie? What would he want to ask me? I don't even know him."

Nick dove right into his story. Actually, Jimmie hadn't asked. The idea had just popped into Nick's head. But it seemed like a good one. "Jimmie, he's going to do a tightrope-walking exhibition at the Independence Day celebration and us boys, we're going to pass the hat. If Jimmie gets enough money, he's going off to join the Sells Brothers' Circus. He'll probably want to write me a letter now and then to let our mum and me know how he is. So I thought, I mean, Jimmie and I thought maybe he could send the letters to you at Doc Bellows's house. Then you could let me know, but our stepfather wouldn't find out."

Loua listened quietly, watching Nick's face with her big, brown eyes. Then she nodded. "Of course. It's a very good idea."

Nick grinned. She thought his idea was very good! He thought she was very pretty. And nice, too.

"Thanks again for walking me home. Just the thought of Tanny-bum sets me to shivering." They had reached the steps at the doctor's brick house, the only house in Fayette made of brick. Too soon, Nick thought.

"Sure. Well, see you 'round."

"See you round like a ball." She giggled.

Nick tried to join in the joke. "See you round like a hoop."

"See you round like the moon," she said.

Nick looked up and, sure enough, the moon was big and pale and round, hanging over the trees. He hadn't noticed before. "See you round ...," he fumbled, trying to think of something else that was round. A marble? An apple? No, apples weren't exactly round.

Loua laughed. "Good night, Nick." She ran up the steps and disappeared through the door.

Nick shoved his hands down into his pockets and headed back toward town. Round like a pearl! That's what he should have said. Round like a pearl, and shiny, glowing, pretty, just like Loua herself. Why did he always think of things too late?

Chapter 11

When he reached the center of town, Nick heard men's voices from the porch that ran the entire length of the front of the hotel. As he came closer, he could see in the dusk that a small group of men had gathered there. In their midst, smoking a long cigar, was Professor Loomis, laughing and gesturing. Nick thought for a moment of edging up and asking the Professor how long it had taken him to teach the dogs those tricks. He'd need to know that when someday he got a dog of his own. But he thought that probably the men would not appreciate him barging in. Maybe he'd have another chance to talk to the Professor before he left town on the next train or schooner. He cut behind the hotel, looking left and right, on the lookout for a tall figure with a scraggly gray beard and wearing a long overcoat even on a warm summer night. He didn't see Tanny-bum anywhere.

But, when he reached the back of the

hotel, he did see something that grabbed his attention. Three wire cages had been placed against the back wall of the building. Dog cages. And in them he recognized the dogs from Professor Loomis's Dog Circus. He stopped at the first cage and saw the padlock on the door. Three dogs lay resting on a bed of straw. He tried to remember what each one had done in the professor's act. One had been the mother and one the baby in the carriage. The other had walked on top of the ball. In the second cage, four dogs rested—the acrobat dog, the narrow plank walker that had reminded him of Jimmie, the can-can dancers and the hoop jumpers. In the third cage, there was only one dog. The small black and white dog that had jumped through the fiery hoop lay on its side. It whimpered softly as Nick, putting his hand to the cage and wiggling a few fingers between wires, tried to reach the dog. He couldn't. The dog was just two inches too far from the edge of the cage.

The dog whimpered again. "Hey, boy, it's okay. I won't hurt you. I love dogs. And you were great in the show tonight. What a brave dog to jump through the fire," he crooned.

The dog shifted and leaned closer to the fencing. Now the ends of Nick's fingers could reach him. His fingertips stroked the warm fur of the dog's head as he talked softly. "What's the matter, boy? Are you lonesome in there by yourself?"

Nick ran his fingers down the dog's front shoulder. The dog jerked away and whined as if Nick had hurt him. He pulled his hand back fast. Looking down at his fingers, he saw something unexpected in the moonlight. Something dark stained his fingers. He touched them with his thumb. Sticky. He brought his fingers closer to his face. Dark, reddish color. It was blood! The dog was wounded and bleeding.

"Oh, jeez, boy. I'm sorry. I didn't mean to hurt you. How'd that happen?" Nick dropped to his knees and got his face as close as he could to the cage, peering at the dog's wounded shoulder. It wasn't a cut, he discovered. The wound was about half the size of his fist—red, raw, and oozing blood. Around the edges, it was black. Charred black skin. "A burn!" Nick told himself. He remembered how worried he had been for the dog as it had leaped toward the flaming hoop. Now he knew it hadn't been needless worry. He also remembered that the dog had not obeyed the professor at first. Maybe it had happened before. Maybe the dog had good reason to be scared. "Oh, poor boy. You need some medicine, some ointment on that burn."

Suddenly, a blinding anger washed over Nick. Anger at the Professor who had put this dog in danger and then not taken care of him. Anger that someone like that owned dogs while he, who would love and protect a dog with his life, could not have one. Red hot anger burned his eyes. "I'll help you, boy, I promise."

A plan was forming in Nick's head. He knew how he could help the injured dog. He knew where they kept the ointment in the stable, a medicine that they used when horses were injured. He grinned as he raced toward the stable. He also knew where they kept the wire cutters.

Chapter 12

Nick sat on the grass and studied the cage. He'd have to use the wire cutters to cut a hole in the cage so he could reach the dog and apply the healing ointment to its shoulder wound. He gripped his fingers around the handles of the cutting tool and positioned the blades on one of the wires near the bottom of the left corner of the cage. He pushed on the handles, but they didn't make a dent in the heavy wire. "Whoa. I'll have to put all my weight into it," he told himself. Standing up, he squeezed his eyes, held his breath, and put the strength of his whole body into his hands. Snap! The wire split in two. He snapped the next wire up and then the next. Sweat beaded on his forehead. He wiped it with the back of his arm. He stretched tall, pulled his shoulders back, and stretched his cramped fingers out, one hand at a time, giving his body a short rest before tackling the sideways wires.

He swiveled his head from side to side,

making sure no one was near. He figured he could probably get into a lot of trouble if he were caught cutting the cage. He heard or saw no one. Pushing the worry aside, he continued to concentrate on the wires.

All the while Nick was sweating, breathing heavily, and grunting to cut the wires, the dog watched him warily without moving. When he thought his arms would break off if he tried to cut one more wire, Nick decided the hole was big enough to reach his arm through. He rested a moment, and then he put his weight into bending the cut wires back until he had a triangular-shaped opening in the corner of the cage.

"Okay, boy." He whispered. "Now I can help you. I've got some medicine. C'mon. C'mere, boy." The dog would not come closer. Nick opened the can of ointment and dug out a glob with his fingers. He lay belly down in the grass beside the cage and reached as far as he could, far enough to gently touch the dog's injured shoulder with the medicine. Then he withdrew his arm.

The cooling ointment must have soothed the dog. He crept closer to the hole, closer to Nick's fingers as they entered again with ointment that he spread gently over the wound.

"There, boy. That should help you feel better," he whispered, stroking the dog. After a few minutes of peacefully petting the dog's soft, warm fur, Nick figured he'd better leave. Who knew how much trouble he could find himself into if the Professor were to catch him here with the wire cutters and a fresh hole cut in the cage!

He stood up, put the cap back on the ointment can, and said one last thing to the dog. "Good night, buddy. I hope you'll be feeling better." As he walked away, he thought that if the dog were his that would be a good name for him—Buddy. If only ...

After replacing the can of ointment on its shelf in the stable, Nick bolted the wooden door and turned toward Cedar Street in the direction of Frank's cabin. He'd only taken a few steps, though, when he heard a noise behind him. Could it be Tanny-bum? Fear made him feel as if he had been turned to stone. He stood stone-still, not sure if he should make a run for it or turn around to see what the noise was. He noticed that when he stopped, the noise had stopped. He took four more steps. He heard the rustling noise again. When he stopped, the noise stopped again. Someone was following him. Anyone he knew would have spoken, not snuck up quietly behind him, matching his steps. His heart was hammering so hard that he thought it might break some ribs, but he had to know. He took a deep breath, got his feet ready to run, and looked back over his shoulder. There was no tall figure in a long overcoat. There was no Professor with a curling black mustache. He lowered his glance and looked down at the ground. What he saw was the little black and white dog. Actually, what he mostly saw were four white paws and the white tip of the tail. In the near darkness, the blackness of the dog blended into the night.

Nick let out his breath in a mighty whoosh. He took a few breaths while his heartbeat tried to return to normal. "Geez, Buddy! You nearly scared the daylights out of me." The dog gave him a soft whine and lowered his head. "Yeah, I know you're sorry, that you didn't mean to scare me." Nick didn't know how he knew; he just felt that the dog would never do anything mean or frightening to him. "But you have to go back to your cage," he said. He stooped and picked the dog up. The dog snuggled into his arms, reached up, and licked his face with a warm tongue. Nick laughed.

Back at the cage, Nick pushed the dog through the opening in the wire. He tried to unbend the wires as best he could so the dog could not escape again. Much as he liked this dog and was worried about it, it was not his dog. He told it goodbye once more and headed for home.

But he'd only gotten halfway there when

he again heard noises behind him. This time he was not afraid that it was Tanny-bum. It was the dog again, and he had opened up his wounds squeezing through the bent wires of the cage. Fresh blood seeped on its shoulder. He must have wanted to get out badly, Nick thought, to reinjure himself like that. It must really hurt.

He picked up the dog once more. "What in the world am I going to do with you?" Nick asked the dog, who only looked back at him with round, trusting eyes.

He sat down in the grass with the dog snuggled on his lap to weigh his options. He could try to return the dog again. But it was getting pretty obvious that the dog would not stay in the cage. It must be bad to be there, Nick thought. He chewed on the side of his thumbnail as he tried to think of what to do. If the Professor mistreated the dog, Nick couldn't take him back. But he couldn't take him to Frank's cabin either. He had nowhere to hide him, no way to take care of him. What, what, what am I going to do? He looked up at the night sky, searching the stars for answers, but none came.

Chapter 13

Even though Nick could tell that the voice came from far away, he could hear it clearly. The anger in it reverberated between the stone and wood buildings of Fayette until it reached his ears.

"Help! Sheriff! Someone stole my dog! Get the sheriff. Look, the cage has been cut. Agh! If I catch the thief, I'll murder him with my bare hands!"

Nick didn't know if the Professor would really murder the person who had taken his dog. He tried to tell himself that he hadn't actually stolen it. But a voice inside him said, "Oh, yes, you did." He would surely look guilty to the Professor or the sheriff, Nick admitted to himself. He hadn't stolen the dog. It had followed him. He had even tried to return it. He was not guilty. But, maybe he wasn't completely innocent either. After all, the dog could not have escaped the cage if he had not cut the wires.

Nick stood still as a statue, frozen, unable to move. His feet felt as if they were cemented down. He couldn't decide what to do. If he took the dog back, the sheriff might arrest him. "Oh," he shivered. "They'll think I'm a thief for sure." He couldn't take the chance.

Now he could hear other voices floating in the darkness over Fayette, and he knew he had to move and soon.

"We'll find him."

"He never came past the hotel. We'd have seen him. He must have gone that way, toward the laborers' cabins."

"Let's go. Let's get the scoundrel."

Nick couldn't see the men, but he knew they were coming in his direction and getting nearer. He had to move. Just had to.

Suddenly, his feet became unstuck from the ground. He turned away from the cabin lane and headed to his left, away from the town.

It was hard to run with the dog in his arms, but he trotted as fast as he could, thankful that the dog was perfectly quiet. Not a single bark or whimper came from him.

Nick kept running, even when his lungs were burning and a hot, searing pain shot through his side as if a knife were plunging into him. He wanted to stop, to bend over, catch his breath, and clutch his aching side. But he couldn't release the dog, and he couldn't stop

running. Staying at the edge of the woods, he raced up the hill behind the school. He circled around to where the limestone cliffs began on the other side of Snail Shell Harbor. Finally, he knew where to go. The cliffs were riddled with caves. He and the dog could hide out in one, at least until morning. He could rest and think. Maybe in the morning he could hide the dog and then find Jimmie. Jimmie was a good thinker and would help him. Or Archie. Archie was a good thinker, too. Right now, Nick knew he was too scared and too tired to think.

He cut across the edge of the limestone quarry and to the narrow ledge of land and fallen rock that separated the cliffs from the water. He couldn't run here. It was too rough and rocky, too dangerous, too many places where he could trip, twist an ankle, or lose his balance and plunge into the lake. He picked his way carefully over the rocks, keeping a tight grip on the dog and trying to listen for sounds that might mean he'd been followed. He heard nothing but waves breaking on rock. He passed up the first caves he came to, afraid that the searchers would think to look there. He went as far along the cliffs as his legs would take him. When they felt like noodles, Nick knew he had to stop. He spotted a narrow cave opening and slipped inside.

The white cliffs outside held a glow in the

moonlight, so he had been able to see. But the inside of the cave was dark as a tomb. He had no idea what might be in the cave. Spiders? Bats? Bears? He shivered and hugged the dog closer, glad of its warmth and companionship. He was certainly glad he wasn't alone.

He didn't want to try to go too deeply into the cave. He was too scared. Also, if anyone came and found him, he had to be close enough to the entrance to try to make a getaway.

He sank down to his knees and buried his face in the dog's warm fur. He concentrated on getting his breathing under control—tried not to think about what might be in the cave, tried not to worry about men following him and finding him, tried not to think of himself as a thief. But, boy, oh, boy, it was hard. Tears slipped down his cheeks and wet the dog's fur. The dog licked the tears from his face. Then, turning his head, the dog began to lick at his wound. "Yuck," Nick said. "That can't taste good. Besides, you need the medicine so you'll heal." The dog stopped licking and settled down, resting his head on Nick's leg.

"Oh, Buddy," he moaned, "what are we gonna do?" He wished Jimmie or Archie was there with him. They'd think of something. But he couldn't. He gave up finally. Sitting down, with the dog snuggled on his lap, Nick leaned his head back against the wall of the cave. Exhaustion overcame him and he dozed.

He didn't know how long he had slept when he was awakened by a noise. He came instantly alert and gripped Buddy tighter. It sounded like the footsteps of a large person, dislodging pebbles that rolled on the rocky ledge. It was coming from right outside the cave. Then he saw a small light. The flame of a match! Its small flame lit the entrance and, for a moment, a tall figure with a long gray beard and a dark overcoat stood in the dim light and blocked the cave entrance.

Nick swallowed hard. Tanny-bum!

Chapter 14

Panic beat like bat wings low in Nick's stomach. He clutched Buddy more tightly to his chest and kept perfectly still. Maybe Tanny-bum hadn't seen him. Maybe he didn't know Nick was there. Maybe he was helping with the search. Maybe he'd go on to the next cave. But maybe he'd find Nick and clunk him on the head and put him in his sack and take him away and he'd never see the light of day again and never see his mother or Jimmie or his friends or the dog. With icy fingers, fear seized him by the back of his neck. Nick squeezed his eyes shut and prayed like he'd never prayed before. "Please, please, don't let him see me." But it was too late for that prayer. Tanny-bum spoke, and Nick knew he's been found.

"Boy?"

Nick cringed. His legs began shoving him backwards, crab-like, deeper into the cave.

"Stop. Stay right where you are, boy!" Tanny-bum ordered.

Nick stopped still. With a swiftness Nick never would have thought possible, Tanny-bum lurched toward him in the dark. Just before he slammed his eyes shut, sure he was going to die, Nick saw Tanny-bum's arm draw back and lunge toward him with his walking stick. He heard a nasty grunt. Eyes squeezed tight, breath held, shoulders hunched, arms protecting the dog, Nick waited for the blow. Thwack! He heard the blow but felt nothing. Then he heard Tanny-bum's deep laugh. It sounded like seven devils laughing as it echoed in the cave.

"Open your eyes, boy."

Slowly, not sure he should, Nick opened his eyes. Quivering just to his right, Tanny-bum's walking stick stood, imbedded. Nick's eyes followed the shaft downward. There, inches from his knee, impaled and dead on the pointed tip of the shaft, lay a huge rat. Nick's eyes opened wide. Tanny-bum had speared the rat and probably saved him and Buddy from being bitten. He was too scared and shaken to talk. He just kept gulping and swallowing.

Tanny-bum hunkered down in front of him. He lit another match and held it up to Nick's face. "You all right?" he asked in a gruff, gravelly voice.

Nick nodded. And then he realized something. "You can talk!" The thought spilled out into words.

Tanny-bum laughed his booming, echoing laugh again. "'Course I can talk. What did you think?"

The match flickered out, and Nick replied. "I never heard you talk before. None of us kids have. They say you can't talk."

"Oh, do they now? And you always believe what *they* say, do you?"

Nick didn't reply, although he guessed he probably did.

"Any of *them* – or you - ever try talking to me? Ever say 'hello,' or 'fine day, Mr. Tannenbaum,' or 'nice weather?' Anything?"

Nick shook his head. "No. We're too scared." He didn't know why he'd told that.

"You'd be wiser to be scared of rats," he pointed to the dead one, "or that Professor. Someone who can really harm you."

It was Tanny-bum who would harm them, all the kids believed. And maybe he still would. But, if that's what he wanted to do, why had he killed the rat? He could have just let the rat bite him. He could already have stuffed him into his sack. Nick was getting all mixed up. "You don't harm kids?" he asked softly.

"Heck no. Why would I do that?"

Nick didn't know why. Why does anyone harm kids? But, strangely, Nick found he was starting to believe the old man. If the kids were wrong about Tanny-bum not being able to talk,

91

maybe they could be wrong about other things. He wondered. "The kids, they say you put children into that bag of yours and they're never seen or heard from again. You aren't going to do that to me, are you?"

Tanny-bum laughed again. "All kids have ever done is cause me trouble. Why would I want to take trouble with me?"

Again, Nick didn't know. Tanny–bum walked back to the entrance of the cave and returned with his sack. He held it open in front of Nick. "If it weren't so dark in here, you'd see what I got in my bag is my supper, a fresh-plucked chicken Dr. Bellows's wife gave me in trade. You hungry?"

Nick nodded. His empty belly squeezed at the thought of fried chicken. He didn't think Tanny-bum would give him food if he were going to hurt him. He didn't think anyone would do that. Of course, the wicked witch in the story of "Hansel and Gretel" had wanted to fatten Hansel up before she cooked him. Naw, that was just a fairy tale. Real people didn't act like that. Did they?

"We'll get a cooking fire going by the entrance, and you can tell me who you are, how you came to be in my cave, and how you got that Professor's dog."

The old man seemed to know where sticks and chunks of wood could be found in and around the cave. Nick followed him out and stood looking back at Fayette, where the glow from the furnace stacks lit up the sky. He wished he was back there on the beach with Jimmie or even in Frank's cabin. Anything would have been better than the fix he was in now. He went back inside and watched as Tanny-bum used a match and blew on the fire until he had a nice little blaze going just inside the cave entrance. In fact, if anyone came, the fire would block his way in. And, of course, it also blocked Nick's way out should he decide to try to escape. It didn't take long for the chicken, cooked on sticks over the fire, to be crackling and spitting and making Nick's mouth water. Tanny-bum handed him one of the sticks, and he brought the chicken toward his mouth.

"Let it cool, or you'll burn your mouth," Tanny-bum advised. He wouldn't worry about a burned mouth if he were planning to hurt me, Nick told himself. He was pretty sure about that. He blew on the meat, trying to cool it off fast. When it was cool enough to touch, he peeled off a chunk and set it down in front of Buddy who sniffed it once and then chewed it up and swallowed. Nick did the same. The chicken was delicious. He told Tanny-bum so.

He had never seen Tanny-bum up close before, so he studied the old man while he ate. Tanny-bum was not a neat eater. Nick's mother

would probably scold him for his table manners, except there was no table. Juice from the chicken glistened on his big hands and dripped down his gray beard. He had taken his cap off, and Nick thought he hadn't had a haircut in many months. His face was brown from the sun, and his eyebrows were bushy. They reminded Nick of two furry caterpillars crawling across his forehead. But, there were crinkles at the corner of his eyes, the kind people get when they laugh a lot.

When Nick and Tanny-bum had eaten their fill, they leaned back on either side of the smoldering fire in companionable silence. To his surprise, Nick wasn't feeling afraid of Tanny-bum anymore.

Nick leaped over the glowing embers of the fire and stepped out of the cave. Tanny-bum did not try to stop him. Maybe he should just keep going, he thought. But what about Buddy? Outside the cave a misty fog had risen from the lake. The air felt wet on his face. He stretched an arm out into the swirling mist and watched his hand disappear. "There's a real pea-souper of a fog out here," he called back over his shoulder

"Ain't safe to be wandering these cliffs in the dark and fog," Tanny-bum said. "I guess we'll be staying the night."

"I got to anyway because of the dog," Nick said.

"Oh, yes. It's time for that story," said Tanny-bum.

As the fog swirled outside, Nick sat down again beside the warmth and soft light of the dying fire. Buddy snuggled up at his side. Sitting there, watching the flames, Nick felt a strange contentment. He almost wished time could stop right then. He'd never have to worry about Buddy or the Professor. Or even other things like Loua Bellows and Jimmie and his stepfather. He couldn't believe that in such a short time he'd gone from being scared to death of Tanny-bum to feeling as if he could trust him and tell him his troubles.

"My name is Nick Stevens, and this is what happened...." He began telling Tanny-bum his story.

Chapter 15

A shaft of morning sunlight lit the cave, falling in a puddle of light around Nick and the dog where they lay curled up on the hard-packed earth. A brown wool blanket was tucked around Nick, making him feel as if he were in a cocoon. He opened his eyes slowly, sat up, and, after untangling his arms from the blanket, stretched them straight up into the air. The dog beside him stirred and gazed up at him. He experienced a strange feeling of disorientation. He didn't know where he was. What was he doing with a dog? His head felt light and fuzzy like the brown blanket. And then the fuzz in his brain began to clear, and he began to remember the night before—the dog circus, the injured dog, the Professor shouting "Thief!", running, finding the cave, Tanny-bum.

Tanny-bum. Nick's eyes circled the interior of the cave, but there was no sign of the old man. He couldn't have dreamed it. Memories of the night before began flooding back. Tanny-bum had helped him, had fed him, had talked to him. Boy, wait until the guys in the club heard about this! But where was he now?

The dog put his white front paws up on Nick's chest and licked his face. Nick laughed at the tickle. "Good morning, Buddy." He scratched the dog behind both ears, which he seemed to like. "Well, I wonder what will happen today. One way or another, I've go to get out of this fix. It's July third. One more day until the big celebration and Jimmie's exhibition," he said aloud to the dog and himself.

"What exhibition is that?" The gruff voice came from the cave entrance. It was Tanny-bum entering the cave and carrying his stick and his sack. He set the sack down beside Nick. "Breakfast," he said as he slowly maneuvered himself down into a sitting position.

Nick opened the sack and peered inside. He saw a newspaper-wrapped bundle. He pulled it to the sack opening and unwrapped it. Spread before him were half a dozen delicious-looking donuts. He grabbed one up, ripped it in half, shoved one half into his own mouth and held the other half out for Buddy. After he had wolfed down two more donuts, he could talk. "I still don't know what to do about Buddy," he said. "Too bad I never found Alphonse Berlanguette's treasure. If I had that money...." His thoughts drifted off to all the things he could do and have if he had money, including maybe buying this dog from the professor.

"Most folks don't believe there ever was a treasure," Tanny-bum commented.

"I do."

"Me, too."

"Really?"

"Yup," said Tanny-bum. He laughed his rumbling laugh. "Fact is, I found it. Right here in this cave."

Nick jumped to his feet. "What? You found the treasure? Here? How? When? What?" Nick's brain was boiling with questions.

Tanny-bum took his time answering, so much time that Nick thought he'd go crazy waiting. "Yup, right here in this cave," he repeated. "Back in a ways. My lantern lit on something golden and shiny."

"Gold!"

"Well, not quite. Golden bottles of whiskey was all it turned out to be. Boxes full. Worth quite a bit of money, actually, if you weren't interested in drinking it, which I wasn't."

"What did you do with them?"

"Took them to Escanaba, a few at a time in my sack, and sold 'em there. Lots of thirsty men in that town." He grinned at the memory.

"That's all? Just bottles of whiskey? No money?" Nick tasted disappointment like bitter medicine in his mouth.

"Nope. Just what I got for selling it."

"Oh." Nick thought for a minute. Then he, too, grinned. "Well, at least that mystery is solved. Too bad it wasn't a lot of money, though. What would you have done with it, if it was?"

"Don't know. I've never had much use for money. I got everything I need."

Nick was amazed at that statement. "Everything you need? It doesn't seem to me like you have much. You sleep in a cave. You trade for chickens to eat. You wear the same clothes all the time."

"True." Tanny-bum nodded. "But I don't need much else. I'm happy. The only difference between me and folks with lots of money is they got more stuff to worry about."

"Well, I got no money and I still have lots to worry about," Nick declared. "If I had lots of money, I would buy Buddy from the Professor today."

"I doubt if he'd sell. Them dogs are his life. Traveling around, doing their act, that's the life for the Professor and his wife, just like my life is the one for me. In fact, when I was in town getting us breakfast, I saw him nailing up some signs that said he's offering a reward for somebody finding his dog."

"A reward?"

"Yup. Two dollars." Tanny-bum ran his fingers down one side of his beard and his thumb down the other, thinking. "Look. You could bring the dog back, say you found him in the woods, and collect the two dollars."

Nick's eyes lit up for a moment. Two dollars was a fortune! Then he frowned. "No. I couldn't do that. It wouldn't be right."

"'Course, you wouldn't be able to buy the dog, though."

"I got something else I need money for— by tomorrow, July Fourth."

Tanny-bum raised one of his caterpillar eyebrows. "Do you now? What would that be?"

In a tumbling rush of words, Nick told him all about Jimmie.

Tanny-bum listened seriously without interrupting. He nodded. "So, that's the exhibition you were talking to the dog about when I came back from town?"

"Yup. Jimmie's got to do a good act. The club, my friends and me, we've got to pass the hat and collect enough money to pay for his ticket to get away and join the Sells Brothers' Circus. We figure he needs about ten dollars for the ticket and eats and stuff."

Tanny-bum combed his long gray beard again with his fingers as he listened. "Yes," he said, nodding again. "Jimmie must get enough money to leave. I'm sure you will be successful."

"I hope so," said Nick. The dog, Buddy, had worked his head into Tanny-bum's sack to find the last donut. Nick laughed at the dog as he tried to shake the sack loose from his head without losing the donut. "But, what am I going to do about you, Buddy?" Same question, still no answer.

Nick went to the cave entrance and looked out over the harbor. Last night's fog had lifted. It was a bright, sunny morning, and it lifted Nick's spirits. Suddenly he felt like everything would work out ... somehow.

"I've got to get back to town. Show my face so my mother knows I'm all right. Maybe find Jimmie or Archie to see if they have any good ideas."

Tanny-bum offered to stay at the cave with the dog while Nick ran back to town. He set the dog down on the old man's lap. Tanny-bum's large hands stroked him gently, and the dog stayed still. At the cave entrance, Nick turned back to check. It seemed as if Buddy trusted Tanny-bum. Nick hoped he was right; he hoped Tanny-bum would still be there with the dog when he returned and that he wouldn't return the dog to the Professor to collect the reward himself.

Chapter 16

Nick stopped by the cabin where his mother, doing the laundry in a tub outside, was hanging the wet pieces onto a line stretched between two trees. The little girls played with their rag dolls in a patch of shade nearby. He was relieved to find that his mother had not been worried. She had assumed he was sleeping outside on the beach with Jimmie as they often did on warm nights. Finding that none of his friends had been by looking for him, Nick set out to find them. But neither Archie nor Teddy was anywhere to be found. Finally, he gave up and went to the furnace to find Jimmie, sure that his brother would help him.

Sensing it would be best if none of the bosses noticed him there trying to talk to Jimmie during working hours, he made his way quietly to the lower level of the furnace where the pig iron handlers labored in the sweaty heat. It wasn't hard to be quiet and unobserved.

The clanking metal, hissing steam, and mechanical noises made it impossible to hear much. In fact, the laborers had to shout to be heard by the men working right beside them. Nick flattened himself against the wall and watched, trying to recognize Jimmie in the dozen men who worked the pig floor. It was called that, Jimmie had explained to him, because of how the iron was formed into bars, called ingots, in the damp, hard-packed sand. The molten iron was smelted, or melted and purified, inside the furnace, fired by charcoal made in the mills and kilns around Fayette by the colliers. As the fiery liquid was drained out of the furnace, gravity took over. The ground from the chutes to the other end of the building was made to gently slope away. Long, narrow trenches, or gutters, were dug and shaped in the damp sand. The melted iron ran down the trenches and out the sides into smaller channels. From there, it spread into the ingot molds where it cooled and hardened into solid bars of iron. Someone once thought that it reminded him of suckling pigs, so the name "pig iron" came to be. Each ingot, or pig, was about two and a half feet long, six inches wide, and three inches deep. Each weighed between one hundred and one hundred and fifty pounds.

Steam rose as the iron cooled and solidified in the sand. Men mopped their sweating brows and used long-handled, hoe-like tools to smooth the iron in the trenches and molds. It was hot, backbreaking, ear-destroying work. Nick could understand why Jimmie wanted to get away from the furnace as well as away from Frank.

Finally, he spotted Jimmie among the smoke-dirtied men and waved for him to come. Jimmie made his way around the cooling pigs and arrived at Nick's side. "Hey, Nick, what are you doing here?"

"Looking for you."

"What for?"

"I was hoping you could help me with a problem."

"Problem?"

"Ah-huh."

Jimmie made a quick, sweeping eye-tour of the pig floor and checked for bosses. Nick looked up sideways at Jimmie. Under the gleam of sweat on his brother's face, he saw a swollen purple bruise on Jimmie's cheekbone. Jimmie noticed him staring and turned his face away. "Can it wait until the lunch whistle? I can't talk now. I've got to get back to work." Distracted, he took a few steps away.

"I guess," Nick said softly. Jimmie headed back to the pigs, and Nick dejectedly left the pounding noise and rising steam of the furnace. Outside, he looked up into the sunshine and breathed deeply. Nope, he could not blame Jimmie for wanting to escape endless days of handling pig iron in there. Escape. Yes, that's exactly what he was going to do. Tomorrow. So why was he so worried about bosses and work today? You'd think he wouldn't care, that he'd be glad to take time out to listen to Nick's problem and not worry about his job since he planned on leaving it tomorrow. Just the way Jimmie was, Nick finally decided. Whatever he did, he would do it one hundred per cent. If he was a pig iron handler, he would be the best pig iron handler he could be. And when he got to the circus, he'd be the best tightrope walker he could be, too.

Nick wandered toward the center of town. He'd been counting on Jimmie or Archie to help him figure out what to do about the dog, Buddy, but neither of them was available. And he had to get back to the cave and Buddy soon. He couldn't hang around long enough to wait for the lunch whistle. He jammed his hands into his pockets and stubbed his toes into the dirt as he made his way slowly toward the hotel. On the wooden siding of the store building, he saw the flier nailed up, advertising a two dollar reward for the return of a small black and white dog, the star of Professor Loomis's Traveling Dog Circus. Contact the Professor at the Fayette Hotel.

As he neared the hotel, he saw that the benches across the front porch were full as usual. Among the men sitting there talking and smoking was the Professor. Nick was interested in what he was thinking and saying this morning about the missing dog. He would have to put off returning to the cave for a few minutes longer while he tried to find out.

Deep down in his pants pocket Nick fingered a few of his marbles, running them through his fingers over and over with his right hand and chewing on his left thumbnail while he thought. He decided to do what he and his friends often did when they wanted to catch up on the town news. He would pretend to be playing marbles in the dirt in front of the hotel, where he could eavesdrop on the men's conversation. It was amazing how adults didn't seem to notice that the boys would be listening in while they played their game. It was as if they were invisible.

With his fingers, Nick dug a small depression in the sand, smoothing out the edges and the sand around it. He stooped down and spilled out his marbles. He would practice his shots. Putting the fingernail of his pointer finger against the pad of his thumb, he flicked the finger against his yellow cat's-eye marble and watched as it hit the blue one and sent it rolling toward the hole. He kept his eyes on the marbles, but his concentration was all on the conversation on the porch.

"Can't imagine where that dog could have got to," one of the men declared, spitting tobacco juice into the brass spittoon beside his feet.

The Professor frowned. "Someone stole him. That's where he got."

"Maybe he just ran away," another suggested.

"Never!" The Professor could not believe that. "My little Toby would never run away. He's our star. He's our sweet little pet. The wife and I never had any children, so those dogs, why, they're just like our babies. Especially Toby. The wife just dotes on him. Why, he eats better than me. I tell you, she's heartsick this morning. Just lying up in our room crying her eyes out. That's why I offered the reward. If we don't get little Toby back," he shook his head sadly, "I just don't know what we'll do."

Nick flicked a marble and sent it flying through the air, overshooting the hole by two feet. His hand shook. The professor and his wife loved the dog. They treated it like a baby. Was it possible they hadn't abused Buddy? Maybe he had jumped to a wrong conclusion. Toby. His name was Toby. Each truth was like a nail pounded into his heart.

"You staying in Fayette 'til you find him?" someone asked.

The Professor nodded. "My wife would never leave without her little Toby, especially since he got hurt. Burned his shoulder. Last show we did, over to Manistique, just when he was starting his leap through the fire hoop, some fool outside shot off a gun. Distracted Toby, well, everybody, actually, and his jump was just a wee bit off. She's been nursing him special. Puts medicine on it, but it hasn't been healing as well as it should because the foolish dog keeps licking it off." The Professor laughed fondly. His voice trailed off. "Just don't know what we'll do ...."

Nick hung his head. He brought his fist up to his mouth and started biting on all his fingernails until they hurt, hurt as much as he was hurting inside. But probably not as much as the Professor and his wife were hurting. He imagined how he would feel if Buddy really were his dog and someone came along and stole him.

Nick stood up and brushed the dirt from his pants. He picked up his marbles and started to run. Suddenly, he knew exactly what he was going to do about Buddy.

Chapter 17

Back at the cave, Nick found both Tanny-bum and Buddy sitting dozing in the sun outside the entrance.

"Hey, Buddy! Hey, Tanny—ah, Mr. Tannenbaum."

They both lifted their eyes to him. Barking excitedly, Buddy jumped up, ran to him, and leaped at Nick as he bent to catch the dog. He rubbed behind Buddy's ears while the dog licked his face. "Did you miss me? Are you glad to see me, boy?"

"Ha! Slept the whole time you were gone," Tanny-bum said. "Probably just looking for food."

"Well, he needs lots of rest and good food while he's healing," Nick explained. He checked the dog's shoulder, and it seemed to him that it looked better today, turning pink and healthy looking.

"Did you find your friends?"

"Nope."

"Decide what you're going to do?"

"Yes." Nick took a deep breath. "I heard the Professor talking to some men about Buddy, only he called him Toby. Seems like he and his wife really love Buddy. I guess I should give him back."

"Yeah. Probably be a lot of trouble to have that dog."

Nick nodded. "He probably eats a lot."

"Yup. Probably chases cats and runs after horses and wagons."

"Ah-huh. Probably wants to do tricks, not anything useful."

"Yup. Probably got fleas, too."

"He does not!" Nick shouted.

Tanny-bum laughed. "You sure you want to give him back?"

"No. I am sure I don't want to. But I have to. He doesn't belong to me. He belongs to Professor Loomis and Mrs. Loomis, and they love him .... Maybe someday I'll be able to have a dog of my own." He kept talking because he was afraid that, if he stopped talking, he'd start crying.

He scooped the dog up and looked toward the town. Then he looked back at the old man sitting in the sun. "Thanks for your help," he said.

"Don't mention it."

"No, really, thanks...."

"I mean it. Don't mention it. To your friends. I've been sitting here in the sun thinking. I've been thinking that probably it's good that the kids are a little scared of me. That way I don't get bothered. I think I'd like to keep it that way. So, how about if you keep my secrets and I keep yours?"

"It's a deal," Nick said.

Tanny-bum stuck out a big, brown hand, and Nick put his into it. They shook.

"It's a deal," Tanny-bum repeated.

Nick picked up the dog and gave Tanny-bum a long look. The old man wiggled one of his caterpillar eyebrows and winked. Nick turned and headed back to town.

The Professor was still sitting on the hotel's porch as he approached. When he saw Nick coming, carrying his dog, he jumped up and ran toward him. "You found him! You found my Toby. Oh, wait until my wife hears he's back." He stretched his arms out, and Nick handed the dog over to him. The Professor cuddled the dog. The dog lifted his head up and licked the Professor's face joyfully. The Professor's mouth stretched into a wide smile as his dark eyes sparkled. Nick's heart sank lower and lower. It was really happening. He was really losing Buddy. He couldn't believe he'd had the dog for less than a day and already loved him so much. He tried to smile at the

113

Professor, but it felt as sad as a smile could be.

The Professor turned to one of the men on the hotel porch. "Go to room seven and get Mrs. Loomis. Tell her Toby is back!" The Professor was happily bouncing the dog up and down. Then he turned his attention back to Nick. "Thank you, son. Thank you so much," he said, eyes moist.

Nick remembered his manners. "You're welcome."

"Now, about your reward," the Professor began.

"No, sir. I don't want the reward."

"What? No reward? Why not? You deserve it for finding Toby and bringing him back to us. How did you find him? Do you know who the thief is who cut the fence and stole him?"

Nick hung his head. He watched his toes curling in the dirt, not wanting to look the Professor in the eye. Moments ticked by.

A commotion at the hotel's door made Nick lift his eyes. The Professor's wife, black cape flapping, swooped down on them. "Oh, my baby! My precious Toby, you've come back." At the sound of her voice, the dog began yipping excitedly. He jumped out of the Professor's grip and landed in his wife's welcoming arms. She squeezed him to her ample bosom, smothering him with kisses, tears, and baby talk.

"Give the boy his reward," she told her husband, as she headed up the five steps to the hotel's porch and entrance, ignoring the sign beside the door that said, "No animals allowed."

"About the reward, son," the Professor said again, taking out his wallet.

"It ... it was me that took the dog." Nick was trying not to blubber, but he had to tell the truth.

The smile disappeared from the Professor's face. Waiting for an explanation, he put his hands on his hips and stared hard at Nick. Any minute now Nick expected the Professor to grab him and call for the sheriff. He began talking fast, spouting out as many words as he could before he took a breath.

"But I didn't steal him. I was petting him and I noticed his burn and I got some ointment and I couldn't reach to put it on him, so I cut the wire. I was just trying to help him. Then he got out and he followed me and I heard someone yelling "thief" and I got scared and I ran off. We hid all night 'cause I was thinking maybe you didn't take good care of him; maybe you were mean to him. And then this morning I heard you talking and I knew you weren't mean, that you loved Buddy and he belonged to you and I had to bring him back." Nick gulped air. "So that's why I can't take the reward. Are you gonna call the sheriff?"

The Professor stared down at him for the longest moment of Nick's life. Then he let a breath out, long and slow. "No, I don't think so. You were just trying to do the right thing, weren't you?"

"Yes, but ...."

"And it has turned out all right, hasn't it?"

Nick nodded.

"Then I think we will just say the whole episode is history."

Nick felt like heavy weights were lifting off his shoulders and flying away up into the sky on little feathery angel wings. He even looked up to see if he could see them. But all he saw were a few fluffy, white, wispy clouds drifting overhead. "Thanks," he said.

The Professor only nodded. Nick stood still but then, not knowing what to do or say, he took off on the run. He'd gone a half dozen steps when he turned back and called to the Professor, "That was some show!" Then he ran for home where Archie had left a message that the Barefoot Boys Club was meeting later to finalize details for tomorrow's Independence Day celebration.

Historic Fayette Hotel

Hotel Lobby

Chapter 18

"I, Archibald Talbot, president, call this meeting of The Barefoot Boys Secret Society to order."

Teddy whispered out of the corner of his mouth to Nick, "Here we go again."

"Everyone stand for the pledge," Archie ordered. The boys stood in their circle. They spit into their palms and rubbed two hands together fast. Then they placed right palms over their hearts and repeated their sacred pledge.

"We pledge our loyalty to the club and promise to solve mysteries and do deeds that need to be done. Criss-cross our hearts and hope to die; we will only share our secrets with the sky."

The boys crossed their hearts with fingered X's and sat down again in their circle on the grass.

"First item, old business," Archie intoned. "Anyone have anything to report?"

Oh, boy, do I ever, Nick thought. "The

mystery of Alphonse Berlanguette's treasure has been solved."

"What?" all the boys chorused.

"Tanny-bum actually found what Berlanguette had hidden in one of the caves."

"Gold? Money? Jewels?" the boys all chimed in hopefully.

"No, just boxes full of whiskey bottles. Tanny-bum took them to Escanaba and sold them. And that's all there was."

The boys looked at Nick in amazement. "How do you know?"

Nick had to be careful here. He had to tell his friends the news so they wouldn't keep searching for the treasure forever. But he also had given Tanny-bum his word that he'd keep his secrets. Finally, he decided to tell them just a little. "Tanny-bum told me. He can talk. He just doesn't want to."

"You talked to Tanny-bum?" Teddy asked, disbelief in his voice.

"Yeah. He ... he caught me last night. I had cut a hole in the Professor's cage and took the little black dog out so I could put ointment on a burn he had, and the Professor wanted to call the sheriff and have me arrested for being a thief. I got in a panic and ran and hid with the dog. Tanny-bum found where we were hiding, and I was scared to death." That much was true. "I was hiding in a cave, and that's the same one where he found the whiskey. That's why he told me about it. That's how I know."

The boys were looking at him strangely and in awe. "What did he do to you?"

"Nothing. I can run faster than him, and I ran for my life over the cliffs. I hope I never have to get too close to him again!" There, that ought to keep them believing Tanny-bum was fearful so kids wouldn't follow him and bother him.

"Oh, boy, what a night you had! That must have been the scariest, worst night in your life," Joe said.

"Ah-huh." Nick nodded. He made an exaggerated shiver. "It sure was."

They were temporarily silent, imagining the terror. Nick felt as if they were looking at him differently, like maybe he was someone special, someone brave. No one had ever looked at him like that before. It was not a bad feeling. Nick decided he liked it, the feeling of being admired. Maybe someday he'd try to do something really brave and important to deserve their admiration.

Finally, Archie broke the silence, and Nick was very relieved when he jumped to a different subject.

"Next item of business, the celebration tomorrow."

"What is the plan for tomorrow?" Joe

asked.

"Well, that's what we're here to figure out," Archie told him. The boys discussed all the things they had to do during the Independence Day events. It was decided that they would meet right after the parade, because Archie would be busy until then being in the parade, riding his new velocipede with the other children of the village who were lucky enough to own a cycle.

There would be speeches to hear. After that, the people races and games would begin. Each child could participate in two races. Nick would be in the sack race, and he and Teddy would partner up for the three-legged race.

Next came the horse racing. Later, during the baseball game, they would sell food and lemonade and the new ginger ale soda pop that came in bottles that Mr. Harris was going to start selling at the butcher shop.

Then came the most important part. During the seventh inning break in the game, Jimmie would do his exhibition, and they would pass the hat for the collection. After that, they would meet Jimmie down at the main dock where they would give him the money, and he would hide until the Garden baseball team boarded their boat to go back up the lake to Garden.

"All right. We all know what to do."

Archie reached behind him and pulled forward a sack. "Now, here's the stuff to decorate my velocipede for the parade. We've got to do a good job and win the one dollar prize money for Jimmie's ticket." They wound red, white and blue strips of crepe paper through the spokes and around the handlebars, and they cut streamers to float out behind Archie on the parade route. Before they were finished, every piece of metal was covered except for the outside of the wheels. While they worked, they decided who would participate in which games and who would take which sections of the crowd for selling and donations for Jimmie. They were all so excited about the next day that Nick didn't know how any of the Barefoot Boys would sleep that night. And, on top of that, it would probably be the last night he would sleep beside his brother Jimmie....

Chapter 19

Nick pulled his blanket around him and wiggled down into the sand until it molded to the shape of his body. He looked over at Jimmie to his right. Jimmie lay gazing up at the stars, hands locked under his head, elbows sticking out. Nick wondered what was going through his big brother's head on this night, probably his last night in Fayette for a very, very long time.

At first, they talked about the day. "What was it you wanted to talk about when you came to the furnace this morning?" Jimmie asked. "I looked for you at lunch time, but you didn't come back."

"I know. I had a problem and I wanted your advice. But, it turned out that it was solved by noon. See, I had a dog for a while, a little black and white dog named Buddy." He told Jimmie all about his adventures with Buddy, Tanny-bum, and the Professor. "So, that's how I came to have a dog for ...." He paused and quickly counted in his head.

125

"Thirteen and a half hours."

"Someday you'll have a dog of your own. You won't live with Frank forever."

"I know. You'll see. Someday I will have a dog of my own."

Jimmie smiled. Nick could see his teeth gleaming white in the moonlight beneath the darker shadow of the bruise on his cheek. Boy, he was sure going to miss Jimmie, especially the summer nights they spent sleeping on the beach. He would miss the talks they had while they watched the course of the stars across the heavens and listened to the waves lapping on the shore. Somehow, measured against the immense darkness, the stars millions of miles away in the vast universe, Nick's usual problems and worries seemed small. And talking them over with Jimmie certainly did help. This time he said it aloud. "I'm sure gonna miss you."

"Yeah," Jimmie said softly, "I'm going to miss you and Mama, too. But, I just got to go."

"I know."

It was quiet for a few minutes, except for the thrum of frogs and the chirp of crickets.

"Maybe you could come, too," Jimmie suggested. "If we could get enough money, I'd take you with me."

"Would you, really?"

"Yup."

Nick swallowed past the lump in his

throat. "Thanks, Jimmie. But, I can't go. It's your life, your chance. I got to stay here and take care of Mama and the girls and go to school and stuff. This is my life. For now."

"You're right," Jimmie said.

"Besides, I think Fayette must be the best place in the world to live."

"And how would you know? How much of the world have you seen?" Jimmie asked, teasing. He knew very well that the farthest Nick had ever been was Escanaba and that only once for the circus.

"Well, not much, I guess," he admitted. "When you get to see all those places, traveling with the circus, you can tell me all about them."

"I will," Jimmie promised. "I'll write." Nick had told him of his idea to send letters through Loua Bellows. "Good plan," Jimmie said. "That way you and Mama will know where I am and how I'm doing, but Frank won't. I want to try to send Mama some money, too. She's going to miss my pay from the furnace."

"I can probably help out more, get more odd jobs," Nick offered.

"But don't you ever quit school, Nick. Get all the education you can. You're smart, and an education will help you no matter what you do or where you end up in life. Promise me you won't quit."

Nick promised. It was an easy promise to make. On the whole, he kind of liked school, liked learning about interesting places and people in the world. "Are you wishing you had told Mama ahead of time?"

"No. Tomorrow's soon enough. She'd only have worried herself and me, trying to talk me out of leaving. And maybe she wouldn't mean to, but maybe she would have let it slip to Frank. Or maybe he would have noticed her acting different and made her tell. No. It's better this way. It's gonna be hard tomorrow, though."

"Are you scared?"

"Of what?"

"Everything. Tightrope walking, going far away on your own, joining the circus ...."

"Yeah," Jimmie answered. For a while it seemed as if that was all he was going to say. But then he began to talk in a low voice. "At first, when I started learning and practicing, it was easy to tell myself that I wasn't any good at it. It was safer that way. But pretty soon I couldn't say that any more. It just feels good, feels right, like it's a talent that I've been blessed with and I feel best when I'm using it. So I started getting more confidence. But, yeah, I'm scared for tomorrow. The way I see it, though, is if you've got enough confidence to try something, then you have to have enough confidence to fail. 'Cause it could happen. And if it does, I'm scared of how I'll deal with it. It's my dream ...." his voice trailed off into the soft quiet of the night.

Nick thought that Jimmie had just said something very meaningful. Something he would need to work his brain over to understand. Something that maybe could help him with his lasting despair over the spelling bee. But not tonight. Not tonight.

"Look! A shooting star!" Nick pointed upward to their left, where a streak of light made an arc across the deep velvet of the sky. "It's a sign. Make a wish on a shooting star, and it will come true." Nick closed his eyes and wished with all his might that everything would work out tomorrow and that Jimmie could live his dream.

Chapter 20

Independence Day dawned with a bright sun and a clear, blue sky. By nine o'clock the population of the whole town of Fayette, about five hundred people, had assembled along the main street that wound between the hotel and the Music Hall, past the stable and the furnace complex, and then up the hill toward the school. There was a festive atmosphere throughout the town. People called out greetings to neighbors, friends, and fellow workers. Older children ran around looking for friends and opportunities for fun. In their excitement, younger children ran in circles around their parents, in and around and between legs.

But when the furnace whistle blew the signal to start the parade and the first notes from the Fayette Coronet Band floated over the town, all gathered along the road, small children on fathers' shoulders and older children in front so all could see the wonderful parade.

"Here it comes! Here it comes!" Excited voices spread the word. Almost jumping with excitement, Nick stood with his mother, Jimmie, and the two little girls alongside Teddy and his family.

And then, around the bend, came their first glimpse of the parade. Two prancing horses came first. Mounted on them were George and Martha Washington. It was really J.B. Kitchen and his wife. Furnace superintendent Kitchen wore white knee britches tucked into tall riding boots, a shirt with white lace ruffles cascading down his chest, and a blue coat with gold trim. On his head was perched a white wig like Nick had seen in pictures at school of colonial men. The long, white hair was tied in back with a thin, black ribbon. In his hand he held the pole of the American flag—not the flag with thirteen stars of Washington's time, Nick noticed, but a modern 1881 flag with thirty-eight stars. Mrs. Kitchen wore a long, flouncy dress of bright red with white ruffles and blue bows. She held onto the horse's reins with one hand and waved with the other. The crowd clapped and waved back as they rode by.

Next came the coronet band of horns and drums played by men in their blue uniforms. The town was very proud of both their band and their uniforms. How many towns the size of Fayette, they asked, have bands with such nice uniforms? They stepped smartly as they played patriotic marching songs. Nick felt his feet moving up and down, marching in place to the music. The drumbeat seemed to reverberate through his body, moving it in time to the music. He wondered if his heart's beats were in time to the music. He suspected so.

After the band came a large, flat wagon pulled by a team of matched black horses. Thirteen of the village's young girls sat on bales of straw covered with sheets. Each girl was dressed in her very best fancy dress of red, blue or white with a banner across their chests with the name of one of the thirteen original states printed on. Nick had to smile when he saw that Virginia Olsen wore the banner of the state of Virginia. Near the back of the wagon, on his side, Nick saw that Loua Bellows represented Massachusetts. She looked so pretty in her blue and white dress with her hair in shining curls. She just glowed, Nick thought, as if she'd been licked clean all over by a cat. She waved and smiled at everyone all along the parade route, Nick knew, but when she saw him standing beside the road, he was sure her smile got wider and she mouthed the words, "Hello, Nick," to him. He waved back, smiling so big that his cheeks hurt. And then the wagon had rolled past, and he was looking at the curls in a big white bow cascading down the back of her head.

Teddy nudged him with his elbow and gave him a knowing smirk. "Loua sure looks pretty today, doesn't she, Nick?"

"Yeah. She looks all right."

"Yeah. She looks all right." Teddy imitated him mockingly. Then he laughed and gave Nick a shove.

"Hey, look! There's Archie!" Nick was glad to change the subject.

Archie, with a big first-place satin ribbon pinned to his chest, led the other cyclists as they wobbled over the rocky, slag-covered road. He wore the Uncle Sam outfit his mother had made—red-and-white striped pants, a blue vest and a tall hat. The brim was red, and stripes of red and white ran up its sides. It was tied around the brim with a wide blue band. Archie looked exactly like Uncle Sam. He had even pasted some cotton quilt batting on his chin for a white beard. When he got alongside Nick and Teddy, he lifted one hand from his handlebar for a moment and pointed to the ribbon on his chest. He grinned as the boys clapped and hooted. They had won the first dollar toward Jimmie's ticket.

The cycles were followed by the Fayette Baseball Club in their gray uniforms. Then the members of clubs and organizations, like the

Oddfellows, marched together. He recognized the red, green and white flag of the Italian Society and the blue and white fleur-de-lis flag of the French Brotherhood. In the midst of the other Frenchmen strutted Frank Demone. As he passed, he nodded toward his wife and children. The girls and Nick's mother waved, but Jimmie and Nick only returned their stepfather's nod. He was working afternoon shift, so he could participate in the parade, but he wouldn't be around when Jimmie did his exhibition. That was perfect, they thought, grateful for shift work at the furnace.

Bringing up the rear of the parade were the sheriff and his two deputies. Nick wondered what would happen if a crime were committed in Fayette during the parade. After the sheriff and deputies passed, the crowd fell in behind and marched along, following the parade out of town, past the school and up the hill to the bluff-top location of the race track and the baseball field. As they passed, Nick and Teddy and their families joined the parade, too.

"Now for the fun!" Nick said, grinning at his friend.

"And the work we've got to do," Teddy reminded him.

Jimmie stepped between the two boys and put a hand on their shoulders. "Have I told you guys that I appreciate what you're doing today?" he asked.

"You don't have to," Teddy said.

"Oh, yes, he does," said Nick, grinning at Jimmie. Jimmie gave him a playful shove.

Chapter 21

The coronet band led the villagers once around the racetrack playing their theme song, the "Fayette Quick Step."

Families and friends settled on blankets they'd brought or on the benches set up along the edge of the track. A platform had been erected in a central spot. It was draped with red, white, and blue bunting. Poles holding the Michigan and United States flags were set into holding pipes on either side. This would be headquarters for the day's activities. Mr. J.B. Kitchen, the sheriff, and Mr. T. J. Streeter, Grand Marshall for the day, sat on chairs on the platform. They would give out the prizes. Mr. Talbot, Archie's dad, stood to the side of the platform holding a megaphone to amplify his voice and ready to make announcements to the crowd.

It began with a welcome by Superintendent Kitchen. Then Mr. Streeter gave a heartfelt, dramatic reading of The Declaration of Independence. "We hold these truths to be self-evident, that all men are created equal, that they are endowed by their Creator with certain unalienable Rights, that among these are Life, Liberty and the Pursuit of Happiness ...." These words danced across Nick's mind. That's what Jimmie is doing today, he thought. Just like our revolutionary forefathers had, he was taking a big risk for the sake of life, liberty, and the pursuit of his happiness.

When Mr. Streeter finished, his words rang in the air for a long moment as they reverberated through hearts like Nick's. Then cheers broke out and the coronet band played the National Anthem.

Next came all the various races. Teddy took a second place in the hundred-yard running race. He won a nickel while his friends cheered loudly. Tom and Mike won first place in the wheelbarrow race and got ten cents. Joe and Teddy competed in the egg toss, but one of Teddy's throws went a little wild and Joe had to dive to catch it. Unfortunately, he rolled on top of the egg and it smashed. They were eliminated. When Joe stood up, he had egg goop running down his shirt and pants. Laughing, he ran speedily back to the village to change his clothes.

Next came the sack race. Nick lined up with about twenty other kids, feet inside the

grain sack, hands holding it up to his chest.

"Ready? Set? Go!" Archie's dad shouted through the megaphone. Nick knew, because he had practiced one day at the stable with one of the horses' feed bags, that if you tried to run, the sack got all twisted and tangled around your legs and down you went. He knew it was best to hop with both feet together, so he began hopping the biggest hops he could. Whew! It was tiring. About three-quarters of the way to the finish line, he felt as if he couldn't hang onto his sack and make one more hop. He stopped to rest for a moment and saw that he was out in front of all the other participants. There was only one boy close to him and that was Eugene Colwell, who was taller and had longer legs. Nick gritted his teeth. He was determined he would not let that snotty, shoe-wearing Eugene defeat him. He put all his strength into his last few hops and fell across the finish line exhausted, but the winner! Another ten cents.

There were other races and games. Nick could hear laughter and cheering and announcements, but he lay in the grass behind the crowd, resting up for the three-legged race. He and Teddy would compete in that race soon. He hoped they would win!

Joe had returned with clean clothes, and Nick heard his name announced as the second-place finisher in the long-jump contest. Another five cents for the collection. They were doing great. Now, if only he and Teddy could win the three-legged race....

Teddy found him, grabbed his arm and pulled him up. "Come on, partner. Our race is starting. They're doing the little kids right now. It's the funniest thing you ever saw. They're falling all over the place. It'll be a miracle if any of them gets to the finish line.

"Good thing we practiced and worked out our system," Nick said.

"Now all we've got to do is concentrate and make the system work," Teddy reminded him.

A few minutes later they stood at the starting line with eleven other two-man teams, ankles tied together with rag strips and arms locked behind each other's backs.

"Ready? Set? Go!"

They were off. Their system was to count one-two, one-two, one-two. On "one" they would step with their outside foot, on "two" with their inside tied foot while trying to keep the length of their steps even. They chanted softly to each other, "One-two, one-two," all the way to the finish line in first place! Another ten cents.

They crashed down onto the grass, trying to free their legs from the knotted rag. "We did it, partner!" Teddy yelled. "We won! And we never fell down once."

Nick was doing the math in his head.

A dollar and forty cents now for Jimmie.

The next race was one the whole village looked forward to. It was the Fat Man's Race. The four biggest men in Fayette could compete for the questionable honor of possessing the wide, fancy, silver-plated championship belt until next Independence Day. This year it was J.P. Jubb, Captain Joe Colwell who was Eugene's father, William Pinchin from the dry goods store, and Captain Olmstead. "Over nine hundred pounds of flesh are entered in this fifty-yard race," Mr. Talbot announced. He introduced each of the men and they stepped forward, dressed in their skimpiest undershirts and short, cut-off pants, clowning and strutting, showing their muscles, but mostly showing off their enormous proportions while the crowd hooted and cheered. They lined up in exaggerated postures to start. Just watching them stand there was enough to make everyone laugh. But when they started running, it really got hilarious.

"Ready? Set? Go!"

The four huge men lumbered down the track to much laughter and cheering. Pinchin was the fastest at the start but, after about twenty yards, he tuckered out and finished the race at barely a fast walk—and dead last.

The crowd teased him as he slowly cantered by.

Olmstead crossed the finish line first and fell flat down on the track. Then came Colwell in second and Jubb in third. All collapsed at the finish, except for Pinchin who stood and thumbed his nose at the crowd. Olmstead had to be helped up to receive the champion's belt. The belt, though, could not fit all the way around his middle, so the sheriff ended up draping it over his shoulders. He bowed like a fancy lady, and the crowd roared.

The boys laughed delightedly at his antics. "Now, that was some race," Nick said.

"I thought I felt the earth shake when they ran past," said Archie.

"I thought I was hearing thunder," Teddy added.

They laughed again.

The horse races were next. Nick figured they had the people races first because the people weren't likely to mess on the track the way horses might. If they had the horse races first, they'd probably have to shovel the track before the people races could begin. Good planning, he thought.

It was a good day for Fayette's trotters. Fayette's "Pet" beat the Escanaba horse in the first race, and "Dick" beat the horse from Garden in the second.

After the races, there was a break in

activities. It was a time for families to visit or have a lunch before the afternoon's baseball game. The boys gave their winnings, the dollar and forty cents, to Archie to keep safe until later, and then they went off to join their families. The 1881 Independence Day was off to great start. "So far, so good," Nick thought.

Chapter 22

The baseball game was everything a fan could hope for. The pitchers from both teams, winding their arms like windmills, threw controlled pitches. The batters swung mightily and got a fair number of hits and a few spectacular catches. Nick could only imagine how much it must sting bare hands to catch some of those fast-flying balls. Stealing bases was not allowed, but base running was often creative, even though everyone tried to keep their uniforms clean. Baseball was, after all, a gentleman's game, and manners were important.

Members of the Barefoot Boys Club, however, were often so busy selling food and drinks that they couldn't watch much of the game.

The icy-cold drinks and food were very popular with the fans and players alike. Each boy had a metal bottle opener for taking off the caps of the ginger ale bottles. The openers were tied to strings and then pinned to their pants.

The bottle openers got lots of use in the heat. Their food items sold well, too— shaved beef sandwiches, hardboiled eggs, and fresh, early strawberries. The boys' pockets bulged with coins. Twice already Archie had come and collected their money. The boys emptied their pockets, dropping handfuls of coins into the metal box where Archie was keeping the money safe with a padlock. When the box got full or too heavy, or when they needed to replenish their supplies, he ran back to the butcher shop, where Mr. Harris and his wife were kept busy making more lemonade and sandwiches. Mr. Harris would go back to the game with Archie, both of them pulling a milk can cart loaded with piles of sandwiches under towels, buckets of lemonade, wooden crates of ginger ale bottles, and baskets of eggs and berries.

Each of the boys had a little stand set up which was made of wooden crates from which to sell their wares. Nick watched as the coins accumulated and thought about how each item they sold earned a penny for Jimmie. He thought all the pennies must be adding up to a pretty good sum. He hoped so, anyway, because it was nearly time for the seventh-inning break.

After the seventh inning, the baseball players would take a rest to get ready for the final push in the last two innings. That gave fans time to stretch, players time to have a drink or a snack, and allow everyone a chance to use a privy if they needed to. And just before the final two innings would begin, Jimmie would do his exhibition.

Nick hadn't seen him during the afternoon. Maybe he was rehearsing back at his practice spot in the woods. Sometime during the last few days Jimmie and a couple of the men from the pig iron floor had cemented two tall pine trees, stripped of their limbs and bark, into the ground about forty feet apart over to the right of the outfield. They had rigged up a rope that was stretched taut between the two limbless trees and held by nail spikes about twelve feet off the ground.

As the sixth inning ended and the seventh began, Nick, glancing over at the poles, began to get nervous. He wondered if Jimmie was nervous, too, or if he was confident. Or maybe a little of both? He remembered Jimmie saying last night that if you had the courage to try, you also had to have the courage to face the possibility of failing. Nick began to chew on his fingernails. Please don't fail, Jimmie, he begged silently.

No one from either team scored in the seventh inning, and it ended with the score tied—Fayette eleven and Garden eleven.

Mr. Talbot mounted the headquarters platform and his voice came through the megaphone. "Ladies and gentlemen, boys and girls, we have a special holiday treat for you today. You will witness an act never before performed in public. Mr. Jimmie Stevens of our own village will perform a tightrope-walking exhibition that will astound one and all. Please direct your attention to the right of the outfield where the rope is set up. If you'd like to see this amazing feat close up, wander down that way. In exactly ten minutes, the show will begin."

Ten minutes. During that ten minutes, lots of people and baseball players wanted refreshments. Nick was kept so busy that he hardly had time to worry. But soon he was sold out. He found Archie and dumped the coins from his pocket into the metal box. "C'mon, Arch," he said. "We got to go watch Jimmie and get ready to take up the collection with our caps."

"First, I've got to give this box to Mr. Harris and get our money. I'll meet you there in a flash." Archie trotted away, and Nick walked with the crowd of villagers out to right field to watch Jimmie's exhibition close up.

He weaseled his way to the front of the crowd and spotted Jimmie standing beside the pine tree on the left. Jimmie had his regular clothes on, but he had tied a red bandana around his neck and had wound his pants legs tight to his legs with twine. A tall ladder was tied to the left pine.

"Here he goes, ladies and gentlemen, Fayette's own ropewalker, Jimmie Stevens!" Mr. Talbot called out.

A hush fell over the crowd, and all eyes moved upward as Jimmie climbed the ladder, gripping it with his left hand, holding his balance pole of lightweight bamboo in his right. Nick had watched Jimmie practicing in the woods several times, and he knew Jimmie was good. But his stomach was in knots today for the big exhibition. So many things could go wrong. He was almost afraid to watch Jimmie. At least in the woods he had made a thick bed of pine boughs to break his fall. Here, he had nothing but the hard surface of the cliff top under a few inches of dirt and grass.

Jimmie reached the place twelve feet up the pine where the rope was tied. Swinging around from the ladder, he stepped out onto the rope. Still clutching onto the pine, Jimmie bounced a few times, testing the "give" in the rope. It must have satisfied him because he brought his balance pole around in front of him, found the center balance point so that the pole stuck out on either side of him and the rope, and took his first step away from the safety of the pine. As one, the people in the crowd seemed to suck in their breaths. Nick could hear "Oooooh!" coming from all around him. He clenched his fists in front of his chest and watched, spellbound, as Jimmie made his slow, careful, one-foot-at-a-time way across the rope. He was amazing! He got to the other pine on the right and put his arms around it. Then he turned his eyes downward to the crowd and grinned. Everyone applauded.

Jimmie took a deep breath, kept facing the pine, settled into his concentrated stance, held his balance pole, and began walking backwards on the rope. It seemed to Nick as if the whole town was holding its breath until he reached the other side and held onto the pine there. When he got there safely, the fans erupted in cheers. But Jimmie had one more feat to perform, his most difficult.

The crowd hushed again as Jimmie carefully made his way back across the rope, about three-fourths of the way to the opposite pine. There he stopped perfectly still except for the slight wobble of his bamboo balance pole as he made adjustments to keep his delicate balance. Then he leaned down, ever so slowly, until his pole was only a few inches above the rope. The crowd was completely silent, every eye looking upward at Jimmie, as he stepped ever so carefully, a bit wobbly, one foot and then the other, over his pole. The crowd gasped in unison. But the pole was

now behind him, and Jimmie had to step over it one more time—backward.

Nick thought his heart might burst as he watched because it was pounding so hard in his chest. But Jimmie did it. He brought the balance pole back in front of him and nearly ran the last steps to grip the pine. He dropped his balance pole to the ground and slid down the pine to thunderous applause.

Mr. Talbot met him under the rope and lifted Jimmie's arm in the air in victory while the villagers cheered.

"Ladies and gentlemen." He tried once more. "Ladies and gentlemen." Finally the crowd quit cheering to listen. "If you enjoyed Jimmie's exhibition, if you think he's as talented as any circus performer you've ever seen, let's give him three cheers. Hip-hip hooray! Hip-hip hooray! Hip-hip hooray!" Mr. Talbot set the megaphone down and put an arm around Jimmie's shoulders. He began walking with him toward Archie's refreshment stand. "Let me buy you a ginger ale, young man." They disappeared into the crowd.

No one noticed as Teddy ran to the announcer's stand and grabbed the megaphone. Mr. Talbot might have been surprised to hear his own voice booming over the crowd as he gulped a bottle of ginger ale, but no one else suspected.

Teddy cleared his throat and loudly proclaimed, in Mr. Talbot's voice, "Ladies and Gentlemen. My son, Archie, and Jimmie's little brother, Nick, and their friends are going to be coming through the crowd, passing their hats for a collection. Any money you can give will help Jimmie buy his ticket and join the Sells Brothers' Circus over in Rhinelander and tour the world. A dream come true for a young man from Fayette who has worked so hard and is so talented. Please be generous when the boys come by. And, Jimmie, congratulations and good luck!"

Teddy set the megaphone back in its place and melted into the crowd to start collecting donations. Nick threw his head back and laughed. Jimmie had a talent, but so did Teddy, he thought, as people came toward him holding out coins.

Nick turned his hat upside down, and people began dropping coins into it. He grinned and thanked them all. But, across the grass, he caught a glimpse between groups of people of the still form and the stricken, shocked face of his mother.

Chapter 23

Nick wandered through the visiting groups of people, holding his cap which was getting heavier and heavier with coins as the townspeople contributed to Jimmie.

Mr. Talbot announced that the baseball game was set to resume, and villagers settled again on their blankets and the benches to root for their team. Nick figured everyone who wanted to contribute had already put money into one of the boys' hats, so he glanced around, looking for them. He saw Tom and Mike already heading for town and the boat dock, their meeting place. He decided he might as well head that way too. But as he rounded the end of the benches a voice called out, "Boy! Nick?"

He turned around and saw Professor Loomis walking toward him. "Yes, Professor?" He waited for the man to reach him and then asked, "How is Bud—ah, Toby? Is his wound getting better?"

"Sure is. Come visit him tomorrow. You can say good-bye before we leave town."

"I will," Nick promised. It seemed like his whole life had become one long series of painful good-byes.

"Here," the Professor said, pulling two dollar bills from his pocket. "You wouldn't take any reward for yourself and I understand why. So, we'll make a donation for your brother. I think he's got a career ahead of him, and it will be a pleasure to help him get started in show business. Someone once helped me when I was young. Now I'd like to help someone else who is just starting out. Here." He pushed the two bills at Nick.

"Gee, thanks," Nick said. "Thanks a lot."

"You're welcome, son." The professor turned and walked back to the baseball game. Amazing, Nick thought, how things work out. He turned again toward the Fayette boat dock, carefully carrying his heavy cap. All along the way he kept swiveling his head this way and that and occasionally turned to look backwards. He wondered if Frank, on his shift at the furnace, had heard about Jimmie's exhibition. If he now knew what Jimmie had planned, would he try to stop him? Nick worried. But there was no sign of him so far.

When he reached the boat dock, he saw that Archie, Teddy, Tom, Mike, and Joe had beaten him there. They sat in a close circle in the shade of a willow bush growing beside the dock, their caps in front of them, counting money. Nick joined them. They were making piles, one dollar in each pile. When all the coins had been put into piles and the Professor's two dollar bills in their own spots, they counted piles. Seven piles and some coins left over. They counted those. Seven dollars and fifty cents.

Nick leaned back and sighed. "It's enough to get Jimmie to Rhinelander, Wisconsin, but not enough for extras like food and lodging.

"Well, Mr. Harris packed some sandwiches for him," Archie volunteered.

The boys were happy that they'd made enough money for Jimmie's trip but disappointed that they couldn't help out with the food. They knew he could always find a place to sleep, even if it was outdoors in the woods, as long as the weather remained nice. But food might be hard to come by.

"Doesn't he have any money from his job at the furnace?" Joe asked.

"He was planning to give it to our mother to help her out like he always does," Nick explained. And, of course, he wouldn't be there to collect his pay at the end of this week. The paymaster would give his pay to his mother.

Nick heard a strange-sounding whistle. It sounded like a bird at first, a sick one.

But when it came again, he glanced in the direction from which it had come. From where he was sitting, he was the only one of the boys with a clear, unobstructed view of the furnace. At the corner of the furnace building, he caught a glimpse of a man with a scraggly gray beard in a cap and a long, brown coat. The man made a come-here gesture with his arm and then disappeared behind the furnace.

Tanny-bum? What did he want? Nick stood up. "I'm gonna go see if Jimmie's on his way," he told his friends. It wasn't really a lie; he could do that at the same time as he found out why Tanny-bum was calling him.

He rounded the corner of the furnace building, and there was Tanny-bum, leaning against the bricks. Good. He could tell Tanny-bum about the reward and Jimmie and everything. Nick remembered something from their conversation the night in the cave when he had first gotten to know the old man. "Good day, Mr. Tannenbaum. Fine day, isn't it?"

Tanny-bum grinned. "Yup."

"Aren't you hot in that coat? It's about ninety degrees out here today."

"Nah."

"What do you want? Why did you call me over? I thought you didn't want to have anything to do with us kids."

"Right," Tanny-bum said. "But I was

curious. I watched your brother's act. He did good."

"Yup. He sure did," Nick agreed, smiling.

"So, did you get enough money together for him?"

"Sort of." Nick explained the situation and told him of the Professor's gift.

Tanny-bum made a grunting sound. Then he pulled a pocketknife out, flipped it open, and reached down to the bottom of his overcoat. He pulled the hem up and stuck his knife into the stitches that held the hem. The stitches popped as the knife blade hit them.

"What in the world...?" Nick whispered.

Tanny-bum reached inside the coat's lining and pulled out three one dollar bills. "Here," he said, handing them to Nick.

Nick looked up into the old man's face in wonder.

"It's from the treasure." Tanny-bum laughed his rumbling laugh. "I guess you found the treasure after all."

"You sure you want to do this?"

"Yes. I'm sure. Now, go on. Get out of here. But don't tell anyone how you got the money, or I'll be back for you." One caterpillar eyebrow rose, and the other eye winked.

Nick nodded but stood still.

"Go, now. By the sound of that cheering up on the bluff, I think the game is over and

159

Fayette must have won."

"Thanks, Mr. Tannenbaum."

Tanny-bum made a shooing motion with his hand and turned away. A minute later he had disappeared behind some bushes at the other end of the furnace wall.

Nick ran back to his friends at the dock, holding the three dollars in the air. "Look! Look! We got it! We've got more than ten dollars now for Jimmie."

"Where'd you get that?" Archie asked.

"Some strange man just handed it to me and said it was for Jimmie. Then he disappeared."

"A stranger?"

Nick nodded. "A strange man." That was true enough.

"Hmmmm," said Archie. "Sounds like another mystery for us to solve." Nick hoped not.

Teddy was the first to see him and call out, "Here comes Jimmie!"

Archie had brought a cloth bag. The boys scooped the money into the bag, and Archie handed it to Jimmie when he got there. "It's $10.50. Plenty to get you to the circus," he said proudly.

"Thanks, boys." Jimmie looked humbly at each of them. "If it weren't for you...."

"We were glad to help," Teddy said for all

of them.

Jimmie stepped in front of each boy, shook his hand, repeated his thanks, and said goodbye. Nick was last. The others wandered off down the dock.

"I saw Mama's face after the exhibition, when Mr. Talbot announced you were going off to join the circus. Was it hard saying goodbye?"

Jimmie nodded, finding it hard to speak for a minute. But then he saw and heard the Garden baseball team approaching and starting to climb aboard the boat. Jimmie looked from the boat back to Nick again. "Thanks again, little brother. I'll write. I'll send letters to Loua at Doc Bellows's so you and Mama will know where I am and how I'm doing." He paused. "Thanks again, Nick." He wrapped his arms around Nick in a hard hug. A lump the size of a baseball filled Nick's throat, and his eyes burned. "Take care of Mama and the girls." He squeezed Nick hard one more time and then turned abruptly and ran for the boat.

Nick stood on the dock waving until the boat was too far away for him to see Jimmie. He ran his fingers over his eyes and cheeks to wipe off the tears.

Dr. Bellows' House

Chapter 24

Nick sat alone on the dock, tossing pebbles into the water, watching the ripples grow wider and wider. Like Jimmie's world is growing wider, he thought. Finally, he brushed himself off and headed back toward the center of town where the potluck supper was being set up. He found the other members of the club and put on a happy face. They were all happy that they'd been successful in helping Jimmie. They'd done a deed that needed doing and had done it well. Now they could enjoy the dinner and maybe even the dance that followed.

Nick stuffed himself with potato salad and corn on the cob, molasses cookies, rhubarb pie, strawberry shortcake, and fried chicken, which didn't taste as good as Tanny-bum's. As he was dumping his garbage into one of the barrels set up for that purpose, Nick spied his stepfather off for his dinner break, talking with another man nearby. He concentrated on listening so he could overhear the conversation when he heard Jimmie's name.

"So, what do think of Jimmie going off to join the circus?" the other man asked.

Frank laughed. "I say good luck and good riddance. About time he got off on his own and quit being a Mama's boy."

Nick stood still, thinking about what he'd heard. Frank sounded glad. He hoped it was true and that Jimmie's leaving would not cause more problems for his mother and him. Maybe it would all work out right. But, he knew it would not feel right to his mother. She would miss Jimmie terribly for a long time, he figured. He made up his mind to be extra good and thoughtful for her.

Dancing followed the dinner with music from the coronet band. Nick wished he could dance with Loua, but he didn't know how to do any of the steps. Mostly, the Barefoot Boys watched the adults and teenagers dancing. Once he saw Eugene Colwell dancing with Loua, and his insides squeezed in anger and jealousy. Maybe he could learn how to dance before the next Independence Day and dance with Loua then.

He chewed on the skin alongside his thumbnail for awhile and then got up the courage to go talk to Loua. "Do you and your friends want to watch the fireworks with me and my friends later?"

"Sure," she said. "We'll bring a couple of blankets to sit on."

As dusk crept over Fayette, people began to stake out their favorite spots for watching the fireworks. The boys found Loua and her friends sitting on two blankets near the water, just past the superintendent's house. They sat down, and the teasing and playful talk began. Then Loua asked, "Did you get enough money for Jimmie?"

"Yes," Nick said, and pushed away the sadness that was trying to smother him. "He's off to live his life!"

And my life is here, Nick thought, in Fayette, helping Mama and the girls, being with my friends and maybe Loua, going to school, solving mysteries, and doing deeds that need to be done.

Three quick blasts sounded from the furnace's siren whistle, the signal that the day was done.

The first fireworks burst in a bouquet of silvery stars over the cliffs, mirrored in the calm, dark waters of Snail Shell Harbor. The reflection in the water made the fireworks twice as good. Yup, he thought, there was no better place in the whole world for a boy than here at Fayette in the middle of this summer of 1881.

Chapter 25
(The present)

Three sharp siren blasts split the air.
From his perch on the cliff ledge above the
lake across the harbor, the noise reached Ty's
ears. The first blast he barely heard. At the
second blast, he became aware. He shook his
head, trying to clear the strange, foggy feeling
behind his eyes. He blinked and then blinked
again. He felt strangely suspended between two
fuzzy pictures. One picture in his mind showed
a dark evening with fireworks in the sky over
the harbor. In the other picture, it was daytime
with the sun shining down on him while he sat
on the edge of the limestone cliffs above the
water. At the third blast the first picture faded
away, and he was left with the second. He gave
his head a quick shake to clear it.

It was the strangest feeling. Suddenly,
he wasn't sure who he was. He looked down at
his jeans and tennis shoes. For just the briefest
minute, his feet felt weird in the shoes. But

they were his favorite ratty old sneakers.

He saw the letter lying open in his lap.
Oh, yeah, the letter from the box of old stuff
he'd found. He was starting to remember. He
held it up closer and read the careful
penmanship.

"July 15, 1881

Dear Nick and Mama,

How are you? I hope things are
well with you back in Fayette. My life
has become very exciting. I had no
problems getting to Rhinelander,
thanks to you and your friends, Nick,
and the generosity of the town folks of
Fayette. I found the Sells Brothers'
Circus right off. I paid for a ticket and
watched the show. It seemed even
better than I remembered. But maybe
that was because I was hoping to be a
part of it.

Afterwards, I met up with Mr.
Crabb. He was glad to see me and said
he'd introduce me to the Sells Brothers
the next day. Lord, I was nervous. I
dreamed about getting to the circus,

but until then I never thought about what I would do if they didn't take me on. I had money enough to get here, but not enough to get home again. I was plenty scared, but Mr. Crabb, he spent the morning with me, practicing. The rope in the big tent was considerably higher than the one between the pine trees back in Fayette. Mr. Crabb said, "What the heck, son. It don't matter if you're five feet up or twenty feet up. You still just got to stay up." Isn't that the truth?

But all turned out fine. The Sells Brothers talked to me some, and then I went up on the rope for them. In my head I was pretending I was back in the woods practicing above my brush pile. I guess I did all right because they gave me the job.

Mr. Crabb left at the end of the week to go to his family's farm in Minnesota. I was sad to say good-bye. I told him he gave me my chance. But he said I gave him a chance, too. Seems we both came out fine.

So I am the Sells Brothers' Circus

ropewalker now. I even got a fancy blue suit and a red cape. Everything's fine. The circus people have been real kind. They're sort of like a big family, all working together and taking care of each other.

So, don't worry about me. I hope you are well, too. Give the little girls a kiss for me. Here's a post office money order to help you out. I'll try to send money regularly. We'll be in Madison, Wisconsin, starting August first, so you can write to me at general delivery there.

Yours truly,
Your son and brother,
Jimmie"

It felt, for a moment, almost as if he were Nick and the letter had been written to him. He felt as if he knew Nick as well as he knew himself. He remembered Nick and Jimmie and the Barefoot Boys and the things they had done in July, 1881. He didn't understand how he knew the whole story. He didn't know if he had fallen asleep and dreamed the story after finding the box, or if, somehow, he'd been able to see the ghosts and experience their lives in Fayette in 1881.

He didn't understand how. But he knew them, knew their story, knew what it was like to be a barefooted boy in Fayette that summer over a hundred years ago. He could hardly wait to tell his brother, Adam, what had happened. And Mr. Munson. Ty would be sure to tell Mr. Munson that he had been right. History was interesting stories about people just like us who lived a long time ago. Mr. Munson might not believe all of it, but he had proof right here in the wooden box he'd found. Nick's box.

"Ty! Ty! Where are you?" It was his friend Eric's voice calling to him.

"Right here!" he yelled, standing up and waving his arms.

"Did you hear the siren blast? We've been waiting for you. The buses are ready to roll."

Below him on the path along the cliffs, Ty saw Eric leading the way. Mr. Munson and one of the parents who had come along on the field trip followed.

"We were getting worried about you, Ty," Mr. Munson called.

Ty refolded the letter and put it back in the stack with the others. He retied the grubby string around them and put them back in the box with the rest of Nick's things.

He waved again. He could hardly wait to show Mr. Munson what he'd found. Artifacts. That's what his teacher would call them. Artifacts from history. But to Ty, they would always be treasures. He smiled to think that he had found Nick's treasures. Treasures from a time and a place he would never forget. Treasures from Nick and the Barefoot Boys of Fayette.

Sources

Friggins, Thomas, <u>Fayette Historic Townsite</u>, second edition. 2000. Michigan Historic Center, Michigan Department of State. Lansing, Michigan.

Langelle, J.H., <u>Snail Shell Harbor</u>. 2001. Bridgewater Classics. Bridgewater Publishing. Caledonia, Michigan. Reprint of original published by Henry Holt Publishing, 1870.

May, George S. <u>Pictoral History of Michigan: The Early Years</u>. William B. Eerdmans Publishing Company. Grand Rapids, Michigan. 1967.

<u>History of the Upper Peninsula of Michigan</u>. The Western Historical Company. Chicago, Illinois. 1883. Reissued by The Mid-Peninsula Library Federation. Iron Mountain, Michigan. 1972.

Deo, Jack. Superior View Photography Studio. Marquette, Michigan, interview.

Friggins, Thomas. Michigan Mining Industry Museum Director, Negaunee, Michigan, interview and museum archives.

Laakso, Brenda. Historian, Michigan Historical Center, Fayette Historic State Park, Garden, Michigan. Interview and park archives.

Halsey, Dr. John. State Archeologist, Michigan, talk "Two thousand years at Snail Shell Harbor."

Scullion, James. Railroad historian, interview.

Author's Notes

In 1867, Mr. Fayette Brown first saw a grand site on the Garden Peninsula in Upper Michigan. Immediately, he knew he had found the spot he'd been searching for. It was the perfect place to build a smelting furnace for the Jackson Iron Company. The site had the three things he needed most. The first was a seemingly endless supply of hardwood forests from which to make charcoal to fire the furnace. The second was an expanse of limestone cliffs to provide flux, a necessary ingredient in the smelting process for making iron. And third was a beautiful, deep harbor shaped like a snail's shell, which would provide shipping access to the Great Lakes and the steel mills to the east in places like Pittsburgh, Pennsylvania. Brown immediately started the blast furnace operation, which eventually brought 500 residents to the town of Fayette, which was named after him.

For twenty-four years (from December 25,1867 to December 1, 1890), Fayette produced pig iron for the steel industry. It took one cord (a stack four feet by four feet by eight feet) of hardwood to produce fifty bushels of charcoal and one hundred bushels of charcoal to make one ton of pig iron. But the hardwood forests were not endless. As the trees were cut and burned to make charcoal, lumbermen had to go farther and farther away from Fayette to find more trees. Then they had to transport the charcoal back to the furnace at Fayette. It became more and more expensive to make iron at Fayette. Within a ten-mile radius of Fayette, the Garden Peninsula, once covered with hardwood forests, soon became cleared, rolling farmland.

In the meantime, a new smelting process, using coal to make coke to fire the smelting furnaces, was being developed in Pittsburgh. This became a more efficient and less expensive way to make iron. Fayette's future was doomed. In the twenty-four years of its existence as a furnace town, though, Fayette produced 229,288 tons of iron. On December 1, 1890, the furnace was shut down permanently, and the town of Fayette died. Some say it became a ghost town almost overnight.

Like the mythical phoenix, Fayette rose from the ashes. In 1959 the State of Michigan made a land trade with the Mead Paper Company, and Fayette became a state park. Restoration of the town site soon began. Today, it is a popular state park with modern camping facilities, a visitors' center, and restored buildings with exhibits and living history where visitors can learn and imagine what it would have been like to live there during Fayette's boom years.

This story is my imaginings of what it would have been like. When I visited Fayette Historic State Park and saw the photograph of the furnace workers with the barefoot boys lined up in front, I knew I wanted to try to tell the story of Fayette through their eyes.

Nick and his friends and family are characters from my imagination. Tanny-bum is a real character but not from Fayette. He is from stories told to me by an elderly friend, stories of her childhood. But, J. B. Kitchen really was furnace superintendent. Doc Bellows really had a granddaughter named Loua who came to live with him. Alphonse Berlanguette and the debate over the existence of his treasure really existed. Professor Loomis's Dog Circus visited Fayette, and the Sells Brothers' Circus played in Escanaba, Michigan, and Rhinelander, Wisconsin.

The events of the Fourth of July activities are reported in newspapers from July, 1881, and I have tried to report them accurately. A young man named Jimmie Stevens really did do a ropewalking exhibition in 1881, Pet and Dick really did win the horse races, and, best of all, Captain Olmstead won the Fat Man Race. I wish I could have seen it!

R.H.

About the Author

Ragene Henry lives a double life. By day she is a fifth grade teacher. By night she is a writer who likes to make history come alive for children. Mrs. Henry lives in the woods south of Marquette, Michigan, where she grows perennial flowers, makes quilts, and practices playing her hammer dulcimer. Other books written by Mrs. Henry are *The Time of Shining Rocks*, *An Enduring Christmas* and *The Time of the Copper Moon*.

About the Illustrator

Carolyn R. Stich's illustrations capture the wonderful characters in Henry's *The Barefoot Boys of Fayette*. Known for her attention to detail and expressive characterization, Stich has received recognition for her work throughout Michigan. Other books illustrated by Carolyn Stich are Andy Gregg's *Paul Bunyan and the Winter of the Blue Snow*; Shirley Neitzel's *Liberty and Justice for All*, and Jane Stroschin's *Atsa and Ga*, a Story from the High Desert. Married and the mother of two children, Carolyn resides in Holland, Michigan.
www.carolynstich.com

Company Office

Townhall

Company Store

Machine Shop